time is priceless. Which is why in this, her latest
book, Donna Hay has assembled 177 deliciously
easy recipes using fresh ingredients in fuss-free
ways. From roast chicken cooked in half the normal
time to simply beautiful desserts in a flash, these
are dishes that make slaving over a hot stove a thing
of the past. Along with more familiar favourites
there are great new dishes influenced by the
flavours of Asia and the Pacific Rim. Whether you're
creating a celebratory meal for family and friends or
cooking dinner for yourself after a long day at work,
the instant cook provides all the inspiration and tools
you need to make it easy.

"Donna Hay is the new Zen mistress of simplicity in both
technique and presentation. This new tome of delicious recipes
sets the artistic standard for interpretational and beautiful
variations on both Italian classics and new world invention."

· MARIO BATALI

the instant cook

about the author

At 34 years of age, Donna Hay is one of the best-known names in cookbook and magazine publishing. From her Australian base, the cook, food stylist, author and magazine editor has already produced seven best-selling, award-winning books, including *modern classics book 1* and *book 2*, *off the shelf*, *marie claire cooking*, *marie claire dining*, *marie claire food fast* and *marie claire flavours*. This book, *the instant cook*, is her eighth title in as many years. In September 2001 Donna launched her eponymous bimonthly magazine, which became an instant hit with readers. *donna hay magazine* is Australia's fastest growing food title, and is carried by stockists in the US, Canada and UK. Donna's unique approach to cooking is also seen weekly in her columns for the Sunday editions of News Limited's Australian newspapers. She also produces a weekly column for a leading New Zealand newspaper.

thank you

As the title suggests, time seems to be an issue for all of us, and it was certainly no exception when it came to putting this book together. My sincerest thanks to all the people who helped along the way. Con Poulos, for someone with whom I spend much of my working week you continue to surprise me with your talent – it just keeps growing. I know I drive you crazy most days, but if it wasn't for you I just don't think I could have finished half the books I have attempted. You continue to have the ability to add that something special – and 'I'll be the judge of that!'. Ann Gordon, for your fantastic talent in redesigning and refining, keeping the production schedule flowing and remaining incredibly calm throughout. You truly are the No Drama Queen and I just can't thank you enough. Carrie Hutchinson, your talent as an editor cannot be faulted, the added value of your personality and humour is the biggest bonus – thank you. The back-up from Justine Poole and Steve Pearce in the kitchen has been truly remarkable. Juggling a book and magazines in our kitchen and studio is difficult enough without being short-staffed. Only these two crazies would look at this as a challenge and get straight into creating a testing system and shooting schedule. Thank you from the bottom of my heart. Thank you also to the following people: Kate Murdoch for making a comeback appearance in the kitchen to help us get through. Sonia Greig for all your help. Tom Frawley for coming in for a day and staying until the book was done. To my style goddesses Vanessa Austin and Lucy Weight for unearthing the most beautiful props around. Scott Williams for turning up the volume on all things marketing. Jana Frawley, Michaela Cook and all the staff at *donna hay magazine*. Brian Murray, Shona Martyn, Jim Demetriou, Helen Littleton and Jill Donald from HarperCollins. Thank you to our produce suppliers – Murdoch Produce, Paddington and Broadway Fresh Foods and Demcos – and prop suppliers – Waterford Wedgwood, Hale Imports, Bodum Homewares, Design Mode International, Indeco Boards Australia, The Art of Wine and Food, Rhubarb Homewares, Villeroy and Boch, Royal Doulton, Chefs Warehouse, Simon Johnson, Alex Liddy, Tomkin Australia, G&C Ventura, Bison Home, Stoneage Ceramics, Orrefors Kosta Boda, Studio Imports, Manon, The Bay Tree, Country Road and Empire III – and kitchen suppliers – Smeg, Sunbeam and Braun. Love to friends and colleagues for their moments of inspiration and support: Jo, Nicky, Sibella, Niamh and Jenn. And also to my family for all their support. Finally, a huge thank you to my partner Bill and son Angus, who make life so much sweeter.

Fourth Estate
An imprint of HarperCollins*Publishers*

First published in Australia, New Zealand, the United Kingdom, Canada and the United States of America, in 2004, by Fourth Estate, an imprint of HarperCollins*Publishers*

HarperCollins*Publishers* Pty Limited
25 Ryde Road, Pymble, Sydney, NSW 2073, Australia
ABN 36 009 913 517

HarperCollins*Publishers*
31 View Road, Glenfield, Auckland 10, New Zealand
77-85 Fulham Palace Road, London W6 8JB, United Kingdom
2 Bloor Street East, 20th Floor, Toronto, Ontario M4W 1A8, Canada
10 East 53rd Street, New York, NY 10022, USA

THE INSTANT COOK Copyright © Donna Hay 2004
Design copyright © Donna Hay 2004
Photographs copyright © Con Poulos 2004
Art Direction: Ann Gordon
Editor: Carrie Hutchinson
Food Editors: Justine Poole, Steve Pearce, Kate Murdoch
Merchandising: Vanessa Austin, Lucy Weight

Cover: Grilled Chicken and Vegetable Stack. For recipe, see page 83.
Reproduction by News Magazines Prepress, Sydney, Australia.
Produced in Hong Kong by Phoenix Offset on 157gsm Chinese Matt Art.
Printed in China.

04 05 06 07 08 / 10 9 8 7 6 5 4 3 2 1

ISBN 0 7322 8105 9 (Australia and New Zealand)
ISBN 0-00-200800-9 (Canada)
ISBN 0-06-077292-1 (USA)
ISBN 0 00 719690 3 (United Kingdom)

National Library of Australia Cataloguing-in-Publication data:
Hay, Donna.
    The instant cook.
    Includes index.
    ISBN 0 7322 8105 9.
    1. Quick and easy cookery. I. Poulos, Con. II. Title.
641.555

Library and Archives Canada Cataloguing in Publication:
Hay, Donna
Instant cook / Donna Hay. — 1st Canadian ed.
ISBN 0-00-200800-9
1. Quick and easy cookery. I. Title.
TX833.5.H39 2004   641.5'55   C2004-903575-4

A catalogue record for this book is available from the British Library.

Library of Congress Cataloguing-and-Publication data is available on request.

HarperCollins books may be purchased for educational, business or sales promotional use. For information in the USA, please write: Special Markets Department, HarperCollins Publishers Inc., 10 East 53rd Street, New York, NY 10022. For information in Australia, New Zealand, the United Kingdom or Canada, please write to the Special Markets Department of HarperCollins in that country.

the instant cook

donna hay

photography by con poulos

FOURTH ESTATE

contents

introduction

Time, for most of us, is a precious commodity. Which is why, although we all love a home-cooked meal, we don't want to spend hours in the kitchen – or at the supermarket – pulling one together. The solution is to have at hand a range of stylish, innovative recipes that you can choose from, whether you're preparing a quick post-work supper for yourself or a special lunch for friends and family. So, for *the instant cook*, I've brought together some of my favourite dishes, all made from fresh, simple ingredients prepared in fuss-free ways. Each chapter also has insider tips on the short cuts you can take to ensure you'll never again be stuck for an answer when asked, 'What's for dinner?' Instead, with an entirely new selection of recipes to add to your repertoire, you'll be creating memorable meals in minimum time.

soup

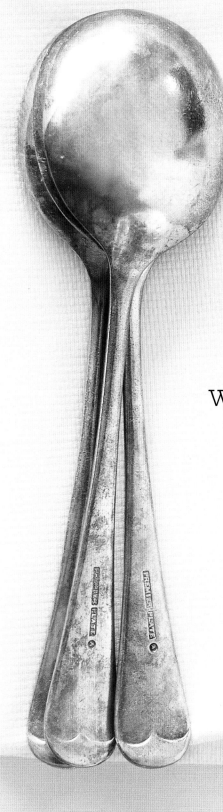

warming signs
How can soup have been overlooked as a meal in its own right for so long? A steaming pot on top of the stove, bubbling with fresh flavour and satisfying goodness, is perfect for lifting the spirit after a long, tiring day. Whether chunky with vegetables and noodles or blended velvet smooth, you won't want to stop at one bowl.

creamy potato and smoked salmon soup

red lentil, carrot and cumin soup

bacon, potato and spinach soup

simple fresh tomato soup

creamy potato and smoked salmon soup

2 teaspoons vegetable oil
1 leek, chopped
2 potatoes (900g/1¾ lb), peeled and chopped
4 cups (2 pints) chicken stock
3 cups (24 fl oz) milk
1½ tablespoons chopped dill
3 tablespoons lemon juice
150g (5 oz) sliced smoked salmon, roughly chopped
sea salt and cracked black pepper

Place the oil and leek in a saucepan over medium-high heat
and cook for 4 minutes or until soft. Add the potatoes and
stock, cover and simmer for 8 minutes or until the potatoes
are tender. Place the mixture in a food processor or blender
and blend until smooth. Return the mixture to the saucepan,
add the milk, dill and lemon juice and heat until hot. Stir
through the salmon, salt and pepper and serve. Serves 4.

red lentil, carrot and cumin soup

2 teaspoons vegetable oil
1 onion, finely chopped
2 teaspoons ground cumin
1 cup (200g/7 oz) red lentils, rinsed
4 cups (2 pints) chicken or vegetable stock
3 cups (24 fl oz) boiling water
3 carrots, peeled and grated
1 tablespoon lemon juice
2 tablespoons roughly chopped flat-leaf parsley
sea salt and cracked black pepper

Place the oil, onion and cumin in a saucepan over high heat
and cook for 2 minutes. Add the lentils, stock and water,
cover and cook for 5 minutes. Add the carrots and cook,
covered, for a further 4 minutes or until the carrots are tender.
Stir through the lemon juice, parsley, salt and pepper. Ladle
the soup into bowls and serve with a dollop of thick yoghurt
if desired. Serves 4.

bacon, potato and spinach soup

6 rashers bacon, fat and rind removed
1 teaspoon vegetable oil
1 onion, chopped
4 potatoes, peeled and diced
6 cups (2½ pints) beef stock
2 teaspoons chopped rosemary
150g (5 oz) baby spinach leaves
sea salt and cracked black pepper
parmesan cheese to serve

Chop the bacon and place in a saucepan with the oil and
onion over medium heat. Cook for 4 minutes or until the
bacon is golden. Add the potatoes, stock and rosemary.
Stirring occasionally, simmer for 10 minutes or until the
potatoes are tender. Stir through the spinach, salt and pepper
and cook until the spinach is just wilted. To serve, ladle into
bowls and top with the parmesan. Serves 4.

simple fresh tomato soup

6 large (1kg/2 lb) very ripe tomatoes, quartered
3 cups (24 fl oz) chicken or vegetable stock
2 teaspoons sugar
sea salt and cracked black pepper
3 tablespoons roughly chopped basil

Place the tomatoes in a blender or food processor and blend
until smooth. Place the pureed tomatoes in a saucepan with
the stock, sugar and a generous sprinkling of salt and pepper.
Cook over medium heat for 6–8 minutes or until heated
through. Stir through the basil and serve. Serves 4.

chicken miso soup

⅓ cup yellow miso paste*
1 tablespoon fish sauce*
6 cups (2½ pints) water
3 chicken breast fillets, sliced
200g (7 oz) asparagus or green beans, halved lengthwise
4 green onions (scallions), sliced

Place the miso paste, fish sauce and water in a saucepan
over medium-high heat. Cover and bring to the boil. Add the
chicken and asparagus or beans and stir to separate. Allow to
simmer for 5 minutes or until the chicken is tender and
cooked through. Ladle the soup into bowls and sprinkle with
the green onions. Serves 4.

chicken miso soup

green pea and mint soup

green pea and mint soup

3 cups frozen green peas
2 large potatoes, peeled and chopped
6 cups (2½ pints) chicken stock
½ cup (4 fl oz) (single or pouring) cream
1 tablespoon chopped mint
sea salt and cracked black pepper
pepper sour cream
½ cup (4 fl oz) sour cream
1 teaspoon roughly cracked black pepper

Place the peas, potatoes and stock in a saucepan over medium-high heat and bring to the boil. Cover and cook for 10 minutes or until the potatoes are tender. Roughly blend the soup until almost smooth and return to the saucepan over medium heat. Add the cream, mint, salt and pepper and heat until hot.
To make the pepper sour cream, combine the sour cream and pepper. To serve, ladle the soup into bowls and top with the pepper sour cream. Serves 4.

VARIATIONS

+ **pea and ham** Add 1 cup chopped smoked ham after blending the soup.

+ **pea and sausage** Slice 2 pork sausages into thick rounds and fry until golden and crisp. Stir through the finished soup for a hearty winter dinner.

+ **broccoli** Replace the peas with 3 cups (300g/10 oz) chopped broccoli.

creamy chicken and cauliflower soup

chicken, white bean and basil soup

tomato, spinach and crisp prosciutto soup

creamy chicken and cauliflower soup

2 tablespoons vegetable oil
2 chicken breast fillets, chopped
1 onion, finely chopped
750g (1½ lb) cauliflower, chopped
4 cups (2 pints) chicken stock
1 cup (8 fl oz) milk
3 teaspoons chopped tarragon
sea salt and cracked black pepper

Place a saucepan over high heat. Add half the oil and the chicken and cook, stirring, for 4 minutes or until the chicken is well browned. Remove from the pan and set aside. Add the remaining oil and the onion and cook for 3 minutes or until soft. Add the cauliflower, stock and milk, cover and cook for 10–12 minutes or until the cauliflower is tender. Place the mixture in a food processor or blender and blend until smooth. Return to the saucepan and add the tarragon, salt, pepper and cooked chicken and cook for 4 minutes or until heated through. Ladle into bowls and serve. Serves 4.

chicken, white bean and basil soup

2 x 400g (14 oz) cans white beans*, drained
4 cups (2 pints) chicken stock
2 cups (16 fl oz) water
3 chicken breast fillets, chopped
sea salt and cracked black pepper
½ cup chopped basil leaves

Place the white beans, stock and water in a saucepan over medium heat, cover and bring to the boil. Add the chicken and stir. Cook for 4 minutes or until the chicken is tender and cooked through. Stir through the salt, pepper and basil and serve. Serves 4.

tomato, spinach and crisp prosciutto soup

2 teaspoons olive oil
1 onion, chopped
1 clove garlic, crushed
2½ cups (1 pint) tomato puree
4 cups (2 pints) beef stock
100g (3½ oz) spaghetti, broken into pieces
8 slices prosciutto*
100g (3½ oz) baby spinach leaves

Place a saucepan over high heat. Add the oil, onion and garlic and cook for 2 minutes or until the onion is tender. Add the tomato puree, stock and spaghetti and cook for 8–10 minutes or until the spaghetti is al dente. While the soup is cooking, place the prosciutto under a hot grill (broiler) and cook for 2 minutes or until crisp. To serve, stir the spinach leaves into the soup, ladle into bowls and top with the prosciutto. Serves 4.

asian pork soup

2 teaspoons vegetable oil
1 tablespoon grated ginger
1 large red chilli, sliced
1 star anise*
1 stalk lemongrass, finely chopped
6 cups (2½ pints) chicken stock
350g (12 oz) pumpkin, cut into small slices
375g (13 oz) fresh egg noodles
300g (10 oz) pork fillet, sliced
¼ cup basil leaves

Place a large saucepan over high heat. Add the oil, ginger, chilli, star anise, lemongrass and stock and bring to a simmer. Cover and simmer for 5 minutes. Add the pumpkin, cover and simmer for 4 minutes. Pour boiling water over the noodles and allow to stand for 3 minutes before draining. Add the pork to the soup and cook, stirring, for 3 minutes or until tender. Stir through the basil leaves. To serve, place the noodles in bowls and pour over the soup. Serves 4.

asian pork soup

prawn, lemongrass and coconut soup

1 stalk lemongrass
2 teaspoons vegetable oil
1 tablespoon red curry paste*
4 cups (2 pints) fish or chicken stock
2 cups (16 fl oz) coconut milk
4 large slices ginger
16 large green (raw) prawns (shrimp), shelled and cleaned, tails intact
2 teaspoons sugar
2 tablespoons lime juice
1 tablespoon fish sauce*
2 tablespoons coriander (cilantro) leaves

Cut slits in the lemongrass down to the root, keeping the stalk intact. Place the oil and curry paste in a large saucepan over medium-high heat and cook, stirring, for 1 minute. Add the lemongrass, stock, coconut milk and ginger and bring to a simmer. Simmer for 4 minutes. Add the prawns and cook for 2 minutes. Stir through the sugar, lime juice and fish sauce. Ladle into bowls, discarding the lemongrass and ginger, top with the coriander and serve. Serves 4.

VARIATIONS

+ **laksa** Replace the red curry paste with 2–3 tablespoons laksa paste*. Add cooked rice noodles and beansprouts before serving.

+ **prawn and bean** Add 300g (10 oz) trimmed green beans and 300g (10 oz) snow peas when adding the prawns to the soup.

+ **chicken noodle** Replace the prawns with 3 sliced chicken breast fillets. Add 400g (14 oz) blanched noodles such as rice, hokkien or bean thread, before serving.

prawn, lemongrass and coconut soup

no-chop vegetable soup

1 onion, peeled and quartered
2 cloves garlic, peeled
2 teaspoons olive oil
1 carrot, peeled and quartered
1 parsnip, peeled and quartered
1 stick celery, quartered
150g (5 oz) broccoli florets, trimmed and quartered
100g (3½ oz) green beans, trimmed and halved
3 cups (24 fl oz) tomato puree
3 cups (24 fl oz) vegetable stock
sea salt and cracked black pepper
¼ cup oregano leaves

Place the onion and garlic in a food processor and process until roughly chopped. Place in a saucepan with the oil and cook over medium-high heat for 3 minutes or until soft. Place the carrot, parsnip, celery, broccoli and beans into a food processor and process until roughly chopped. Add the chopped vegetables, tomato puree and stock to the saucepan and simmer for 12–15 minutes or until the vegetables are tender. Ladle the soup into bowls, sprinkle over the salt, pepper and oregano and serve. Serves 4.

spicy tomato, chickpea and chorizo soup

4 chorizo sausages*, sliced
2 teaspoons vegetable oil
¼ teaspoon chilli flakes
2 x 400g (14 oz) cans peeled tomatoes, crushed
4 cups (2 pints) beef stock
400g (14 oz) can chickpeas (garbanzos), drained
200g (7 oz) green beans, trimmed and chopped
sea salt and cracked black pepper
2 tablespoons chopped flat-leaf parsley

Place a deep saucepan over high heat. Add the chorizos, oil and chilli and cook for 4 minutes or until the chorizos are crisp. Remove from the pan and drain on absorbent paper. Place the tomatoes and stock in the saucepan over medium heat and bring to the boil. Add the chickpeas and beans and cook for 3 minutes. Stir through the salt, pepper, parsley and cooked chorizos and serve. Serves 4.

no-chop vegetable soup

spicy tomato, chickpea and chorizo soup

spiced coconut pumpkin soup

spiced coconut pumpkin soup

1 tablespoon red curry paste*
1kg (2 lb) pumpkin, peeled and chopped
4 cups (2 pints) chicken or vegetable stock
1½ cups (12 fl oz) coconut milk
1 large red chilli, seeded and finely sliced

Place a large saucepan over medium heat. Add the curry paste and cook for
1 minute. Add the pumpkin and stock, cover and cook for 6 minutes or until the
pumpkin is tender. Place the pumpkin mixture in a blender and blend until smooth.
Return to the saucepan. Add the coconut milk and heat for 3 minutes or until hot.
Ladle into bowls and sprinkle with the chilli to serve. Serves 4.

VARIATIONS

+ **chicken and pumpkin** Add 3 sliced
chicken breast fillets to the soup when
adding the coconut milk and simmer
for 5 minutes or until chicken is tender
and cooked through.

+ **pumpkin and tofu** Add 600g (20 oz)
cubed silken firm tofu to the soup
when adding the coconut milk. Heat
gently so as not to break up the tofu
too much. Top with 3 shredded green
onions (scallions) instead of the chilli.

+ **pumpkin and herb** Top the soup with
combined ¼ cup shredded mint,
¼ cup coriander (cilantro) leaves,
3 shredded green onions (scallions)
and 1 large red chilli that has been
seeded and sliced for a flavour burst.

short cuts

from the freezer

Not many foods freeze and reheat well, but soup is definitely the exception. Make double the amount you need for a meal, then freeze the leftovers in single-serve portions. For a quick lunch or dinner after a tiring day at work, thaw and heat gently in a saucepan or use the microwave for a satisfying meal in a flash.

easy mixing

The stick mixer is the ultimate time-saver, particularly if you make soup regularly. This hand-held appliance allows you to puree or roughly chop a soup in its cooking pot, so you don't have to transfer hot liquids into a blender or food processor. It can also be used for preparing sauces, dips, baby food and smoothies.

stock standards

For the tastiest soups, use a base of the best stock you can find. Quality liquid stock can be bought from the supermarket, while frozen homemade stock is often available from delis, butchers and specialty food stores. If you have the time to make your own stock, freeze it in suitably sized portions to use at a later date.

tasty beginnings

Miso paste, red and green curry paste and laksa paste all make great starting points for soups. They add loads of flavour and are especially handy if your stock is not of great quality. Buy them from asian food stores and store them in the fridge after opening. Of course, they're also the base for many curries and stir-fries.

salads

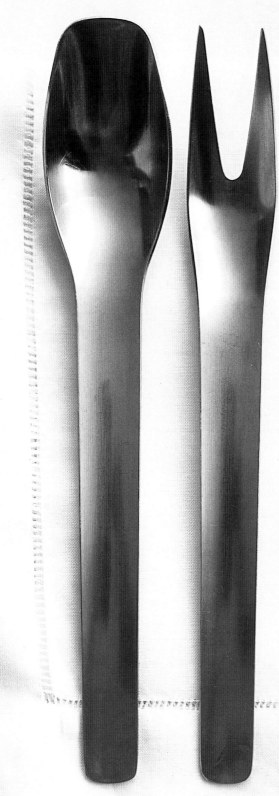

a new leaf
A bowl of crisp greens drizzled with tangy dressing is tempting fare, particularly when the weather turns warm. But there's more to salad than lettuce, juicy red tomatoes and vinaigrette. With the addition of more robust ingredients – roasted vegetables, grilled or deli meats, your favourite cheese – you'll create a meal in no time.

yellow tomato and parmesan salad

lemon, tuna and white bean salad

fennel and blood orange salad

lemon marinated artichoke salad

yellow tomato and parmesan salad

16 small thin slices bread
olive oil for brushing
⅓ cup finely grated parmesan cheese
2 baby or 1 large cos (romaine) lettuce, leaves separated
250g (8 oz) yellow pear tomatoes, halved
finely grated parmesan cheese, extra, to serve
dressing
2 tablespoons sour cream
2 tablespoons water
1 teaspoon lemon juice
1 teaspoon dijon mustard
1 clove garlic, crushed

To make the dressing, combine the sour cream, water, lemon juice, mustard and garlic. Set aside. Brush the bread with olive oil and sprinkle with the parmesan. Place on a baking tray and cook under a preheated hot grill (broiler) for 1–2 minutes or until golden. Place the lettuce on plates with the grilled bread and tomatoes. Spoon over the dressing and sprinkle with extra parmesan to serve. Serves 4.

lemon, tuna and white bean salad

425g (14 oz) can tuna, drained
440g (14½ oz) can white beans*, drained and rinsed
½ cup roughly chopped flat-leaf parsley
2 tablespoons capers*
¼ cup (2 fl oz) lemon juice
2 tablespoons olive oil
sea salt and cracked black pepper
2 small cucumbers, thinly sliced
100g (3½ oz) baby spinach leaves

Place the tuna, white beans, parsley, capers, lemon juice, olive oil, salt and pepper in a bowl and toss gently. Stand for 5 minutes. Place the cucumbers and spinach on plates, top with the tuna mixture and serve. Serves 4.

fennel and blood orange salad

2 fennel bulbs, thinly sliced
2 blood oranges*, peeled and sliced
100g (3½ oz) baby rocket (arugula) leaves
2 smoked chicken breasts, sliced
2 tablespoons blood orange juice
2 tablespoons olive oil
sea salt and cracked black pepper
1 tablespoon red wine vinegar

Combine the fennel, blood oranges, rocket and chicken and place on serving plates. Combine the juice, oil, salt, pepper and vinegar, pour over the salad and serve. Serves 4.

lemon marinated artichoke salad

8 marinated artichoke hearts, drained and halved
2 tablespoons lemon juice
2 tablespoons olive oil
2 zucchinis, sliced
olive oil for brushing
sea salt and cracked black pepper
100g (3½ oz) baby spinach leaves
250g (8 oz) yellow pear tomatoes, halved
4 slices fetta cheese
¼ cup chopped flat-leaf parsley

Combine the artichokes, lemon juice and olive oil in a bowl. Set aside. Brush the zucchini slices with olive oil and sprinkle with salt and pepper. Cook on a preheated hot char-grill (broiler) for 1 minute each side. Drain the artichokes, reserving the lemon juice and olive oil. Place the spinach, tomatoes and zucchinis on plates and top with the fetta, artichokes and parsley. Spoon over the reserved lemon juice and olive oil as a dressing. Serves 4.

sesame chicken salad

4 chicken breast fillets
1 egg white
¾ cup sesame seeds
1 tablespoon vegetable oil
2 small butter lettuces
4 green onions (scallions), shredded
dressing
½ cup (4 fl oz) honey
⅓ cup (2½ fl oz) soy sauce

Lightly brush the chicken with the egg white and press both sides into the sesame seeds. Heat a frying pan over medium-high heat. Add the oil and chicken to the pan and cook for 1–2 minutes each side or until golden. Reduce the heat to low, cover and cook for 5–8 minutes or until cooked through. To make the dressing, combine the honey and soy. To serve, slice each chicken breast into four pieces. Cut the lettuces in half and top with the onions, chicken and dressing. Serves 4.

sesame chicken salad

seared salmon salad

seared salmon salad

400g (14 oz) salmon fillet
2 tablespoons honey
2 tablespoons lemon juice
cracked black pepper
100g (3½ oz) mixed lettuce leaves
200g (7 oz) green beans, trimmed and blanched
dressing
2 teaspoons wholegrain mustard
¼ cup (2 fl oz) olive oil
2 teaspoons honey
1½ tablespoons lemon juice

Heat a non-stick frying pan over high heat. Brush the salmon with the combined honey, lemon juice and pepper and cook for 3 minutes each side or until cooked to your liking. Set aside. To make the dressing, combine the mustard, olive oil, honey and lemon juice. Place the lettuce and beans on serving plates. Break the salmon into pieces and place on the salad. Spoon over the dressing and serve. Serves 4.

VARIATIONS

+ **beef** Replace the salmon with 300g (10 oz) trimmed rump steak and follow the above recipe. Replace the mixed lettuce with 100g (3½ oz) mizuna leaves* and the beans with 200g (7 oz) trimmed snow peas (mange tout). Slice the cooked steak before adding to the salad.

+ **prawn** Replace the salmon with 500g (1 lb) peeled and deveined green (raw) prawns (shrimp). Follow the above recipe, but cook the prawns for 1–2 minutes each side. Replace the beans in the salad with 1 bunch thinly sliced red radishes.

+ **chicken** Replace the salmon with 4 chicken breast fillets. Follow the above recipe, but cook the chicken over medium heat for 5 minutes each side or until browned and cooked through. Replace the beans and lettuce in the salad with 1 bunch trimmed and blanched asparagus and 100g (3½ oz) rocket (arugula). Slice the chicken before adding to the salad.

shredded chicken and celery salad

carrot and chickpea salad   asparagus and creamy brie salad

shredded chicken and celery salad

2 cups shredded cooked chicken breast
6 stalks celery, thinly sliced
⅓ cup flat-leaf parsley leaves
1 cup whole-egg mayonnaise
2 tablespoons lemon juice
sea salt and cracked black pepper
1 iceberg lettuce, leaves separated

Place the chicken, celery and parsley in a bowl and toss to
combine. Combine the mayonnaise, lemon juice, salt and
pepper. Pour over the chicken mixture and toss to combine.
Place the lettuce on serving plates and top with the chicken
mixture. Serve with lemon wedges if desired. Serves 4.

carrot and chickpea salad

1 cup instant couscous
1¼ cups (10 fl oz) hot chicken or vegetable stock
3 carrots, peeled and grated
440g (14½ oz) can chickpeas (garbanzos), drained and rinsed
2 tablespoons roasted unsalted peanuts, roughly chopped
60g (2 oz) snow pea shoots, well trimmed
8 baby cos (romaine) lettuce leaves
honey dressing
¼ cup (2 fl oz) honey
½ teaspoon sesame oil
3 tablespoons lemon juice
1 tablespoon finely grated lemon rind

Place the couscous in a large bowl, add the stock, cover with
plastic wrap and stand for 5 minutes. Separate the grains
with a fork. Add the carrots, chickpeas, peanuts and snow
pea shoots. To make the dressing, combine the honey,
sesame oil, lemon juice and rind. Pour over the salad and
toss to combine. Place the lettuce in bowls and top with the
salad to serve. Serves 4.

asparagus and creamy brie salad

4 large slices bread, grilled (broiled)
100g (3½ oz) smoked salmon slices
150g (5 oz) mixed salad leaves
3 bunches asparagus, trimmed and blanched
150g (5 oz) creamy ripe brie, sliced
dressing
2 tablespoons lemon juice
2 tablespoons olive oil
sea salt and cracked black pepper

Arrange the bread, salmon, salad leaves and asparagus on
serving plates. To make the dressing, combine the lemon
juice, olive oil, salt and pepper. Pour over the salad, top with
the brie and serve. Serves 4.

tomato, basil and olive salad

4 thick slices bread
olive oil
80g (2½ oz) rocket (arugula) leaves
5 tomatoes, thickly sliced
5 bocconcini*, torn
2 tablespoons finely chopped black olives or tapenade
2 tablespoons basil leaves
2 tablespoons olive oil, extra
2 tablespoons red wine vinegar

Preheat the oven to 200°C (390°F). Roughly tear the bread
and toss with some olive oil. Place on a baking tray lined
with baking paper and cook for 10 minutes or until crisp and
golden to make croutons. Place the rocket on serving plates
and top with the tomatoes, bocconcini, olives, basil and
croutons. Spoon over the combined olive oil and vinegar
to serve. Serves 4.

tomato, basil and olive salad

caramelised pear and rocket salad

60g (2 oz) butter
3 tablespoons white wine vinegar
1 tablespoon brown sugar
2 firm brown pears, quartered and cored
½ cup walnuts
100g (3½ oz) rocket (arugula) leaves
150g (5 oz) soft blue cheese, sliced

Place the butter, vinegar and sugar in a frying pan over medium heat. Add the pear and walnuts and cook for 4 minutes or until the pear is just soft. Place the rocket on serving plates and top with the pear and walnuts. Spoon over the pan juices and top with the blue cheese. Serves 4.

VARIATIONS

+ **pear and prosciutto** Replace the rocket with 100g (3½ oz) baby spinach leaves and add 8 slices roughly torn prosciutto* at the same time as the cooked pear and walnuts.

+ **fennel** Replace the pears with 2 fennel bulbs cut into quarters and follow the above recipe. Replace the rocket with 100g (3½ oz) baby spinach leaves.

+ **apple, sage and goat's cheese** Add 1 tablespoon sage leaves to the butter, vinegar and sugar. Replace the pears with 2 cored and quartered green apples and follow the above recipe. Replace the blue cheese with 150g (5 oz) sliced goat's cheese.

caramelised pear and rocket salad

roasted prosciutto and bocconcini salad

6 bocconcini*, halved
6 slices prosciutto*, halved
4 large slices crusty bread
cracked black pepper
olive oil for drizzling
1 bunch rocket (arugula), trimmed
3 roma tomatoes, sliced
2 tablespoons basil leaves
1 tablespoon olive oil
1 tablespoon balsamic vinegar

Preheat the oven to 200°C (390°F). Wrap each piece of
bocconcini in a piece of prosciutto. Place the bread on a
baking tray lined with baking paper. Top with the wrapped
bocconcini. Sprinkle with pepper and drizzle with olive oil.
Bake for 10 minutes or until the prosciutto is golden and the
cheese is just melting. Serve with the rocket, tomatoes and
basil tossed in the olive oil and balsamic vinegar. Serves 4.

spicy roasted pork salad

500g (1 lb) pork fillet, trimmed
sesame oil for brushing
2 teaspoons chinese five-spice powder*
150g rice vermicelli noodles
½ cup mint leaves
½ cup basil leaves
4 green onions (scallions), sliced
2 tablespoons toasted sesame seeds
80g (2½ oz) mizuna leaves*
dressing
⅓ cup (2½ fl oz) soy sauce
⅓ cup (2½ fl oz) lemon juice
½ teaspoon sesame oil
3 teaspoons brown sugar

Preheat the oven to 200°C (390°F). Brush the pork with
the sesame oil and sprinkle with the five-spice powder.
Place on a baking tray lined with baking paper and bake for
15 minutes or until cooked to your liking. Cool slightly and
slice. While the pork is cooking, place the noodles in a bowl,
cover with boiling water, allow to stand for 5 minutes, stir to
separate, then drain. Combine the noodles with the mint,
basil, green onions and sesame seeds. Place in serving
bowls and top with the mizuna and pork. To make the
dressing, combine the soy, lemon juice, sesame oil and sugar
and pour over the salad. Serves 4.

roasted prosciutto and bocconcini salad   spicy roasted pork salad

toasted pine nut and sweet potato salad

toasted pine nut and sweet potato salad

3 sweet potatoes (kumara), peeled and sliced lengthwise
4 roma tomatoes, halved
olive oil
sea salt and cracked black pepper
½ cup pine nuts
150g (5 oz) baby spinach leaves
1 avocado, sliced
dressing
3 tablespoons honey
2 tablespoons red wine vinegar
1 tablespoon olive oil

Preheat the oven to 200ºC (390ºF). Place the sweet potato and tomatoes in a baking dish lined with baking paper and toss with a little olive oil, salt and pepper. Bake for 25 minutes or until the potato is golden and soft. Sprinkle over the pine nuts and bake for a further 2 minutes or until the pine nuts are golden. To make the dressing, whisk together the honey, vinegar and oil. To serve, place the spinach leaves and avocado on plates and top with the sweet potato, tomatoes and pine nuts. Pour over the dressing and serve. Serves 4.

VARIATIONS

+ **pumpkin and ricotta** Replace the sweet potato with 1kg (2 lb) pumpkin cut into wedges. Omit the avocado. Top the salad with 150g (5 oz) crumbled ricotta to serve.

+ **roast potato** Replace the sweet potato with 16 very small roasting potatoes, such as jersey royals. Omit the tomatoes and avocado. Serve topped with 150g (5 oz) sliced blue cheese.

+ **eggplant** Replace the sweet potato with 6 halved baby eggplants. Omit the avocado. Replace the dressing with one made by combining ½ cup thick natural yoghurt, 1 tablespoon lemon juice, ¼ cup chopped mint and ½ teaspoon ground cumin. Serve with grilled (broiled) pitta bread.

short cuts

capturing the flavour

While it doesn't take very long to whip up a salad dressing, you can save a little time by preparing a larger quantity of your favourite vinaigrette and storing it in a bottle in the fridge. This is particularly helpful if you decide at the last moment to prepare a side salad. Give the dressing a shake before pouring.

revival techniques

It is possible to make fresh lettuce, salad leaves and herbs even crispier by immersing them in iced water for a minute or two. Leaving them in the water while you prepare other dishes doesn't hurt either. This technique also helps to revive leafy vegetables that have gone limp in the crisper of the fridge.

make the cut

If you're finding the normal presentation of salads a little ho-hum, try this for a change: halve baby cos (romaine) lettuces or quarter butter lettuces and serve without breaking them into individual leaves. It looks great and allows dressing to collect between the leaves rather than running through and onto your plate.

mixed blessings

Premixed salad leaves offer a great alternative to serving a single variety of lettuce. They come in many different varieties, and with ingredients such as herbs, rocket (arugula) and baby beet leaves, so they can be matched to the style of meal you are preparing. Store in a plastic bag in the crisper of the fridge.

pasta,
noodles
+ rice

pure comfort If you have just one member of this delicious trio lurking in the pantry – and who doesn't? – you'll always be be able to whip up a meal. Pasta, rice and noodles are favourites with just about everyone and they're totally versatile. Mix and match ingredients, experiment with cooking styles, update old favourites… Satisfaction is guaranteed.

mushroom ragout pappardelle

spaghetti with cherry tomato sauce

pasta with ricotta, lemon and spinach

rice noodles in chilli broth

mushroom ragout pappardelle

2½ tablespoons butter
1 clove garlic, crushed
2 teaspoons thyme leaves
750g (1½ lb) mixed mushrooms (halved)⁺
1¼ cups (10 fl oz) beef stock
400g (14 oz) pappardelle
150g (5 oz) goat's cheese, thinly sliced

Heat a frying pan over high heat. Add the butter, garlic and thyme and cook for 30 seconds. Add the mushrooms and cook for 4 minutes or until well browned. Add the beef stock and simmer for 4 minutes or until the mushrooms are soft. While the mushrooms are cooking, cook the pasta in a large saucepan of salted boiling water until al dente. Drain. Toss the pappardelle with the mushrooms and place on serving plates. Top with the goat's cheese and serve. Serves 4.
⁺ Depending on the size of the mushrooms, you could also leave them whole or slice them.

spaghetti with cherry tomato sauce

400g (14 oz) spaghetti or linguine
1 tablespoon butter
500g (1 lb) cherry tomatoes, halved
2 cloves garlic, crushed
½ teaspoon sugar
2 tablespoons olive oil
⅓ cup basil leaves

Cook the pasta in a large saucepan of salted boiling water until al dente. Drain. While the pasta is cooking, place a large non-stick frying pan over high heat. Add the butter and tomatoes, cut side down, and cook for 4 minutes or until lightly golden. Stir the tomatoes and cook for 2–3 minutes or until starting to soften. Add the garlic, sugar, oil and basil and stir to combine. Add the spaghetti and toss to coat. Place in bowls and top with lots of grated parmesan cheese. Serves 4.

pasta with ricotta, lemon and spinach

400g (14 oz) rigatoni
2 tablespoons olive oil
⅓ cup (2½ fl oz) lemon juice
¼ cup finely grated parmesan cheese
sea salt and cracked black pepper
⅓ cup chopped basil leaves
100g (3½ oz) baby spinach leaves
250g (8 oz) ricotta cheese

Cook the pasta in a large saucepan of salted boiling water until al dente. Drain and return to the pan. Place the oil, lemon juice, parmesan, salt, pepper and basil in a bowl and whisk to combine. Add to the hot pasta with the spinach leaves and toss to coat. Place in serving bowls and top with the ricotta and some extra parmesan if desired. Serves 4.

rice noodles in chilli broth

400g (14 oz) thick fresh rice noodles
2 cups (16 fl oz) chicken stock
1 large red chilli, seeded and chopped
1 tablespoon shredded ginger
300g (10 oz) rump steak, trimmed
2 tablespoons vegetable oil
1 teaspoon chinese five-spice powder*
¼ teaspoon chilli powder
4 green onions (scallions), sliced

Place the rice noodles in a bowl, cover with boiling water, stand for 5 minutes or until softened, stir to separate, then drain. Place the stock, chilli and ginger in a saucepan and bring to the boil. Heat a frying pan over high heat. Toss the steak in the oil, five-spice and chilli powder and cook for 3 minutes each side or until cooked to your liking. Slice thinly. To serve, place the noodles in bowls and spoon over the chilli broth. Top with the steak and green onions and serve. Serves 4.

penne with wilted rocket and prosciutto

400g (14 oz) penne
8 slices prosciutto*
2 tablespoons olive oil
2 tablespoons balsamic vinegar
100g (3½ oz) baby rocket (arugula) leaves
sea salt and cracked black pepper

Cook the pasta in a large saucepan of salted boiling water until al dente. Drain and return to the pan. Cook the prosciutto for 2–3 minutes under a preheated hot grill (broiler) until crisp. Set aside. Add the oil, balsamic, rocket, salt and pepper to the pasta and toss to combine. Place in bowls and top with the prosciutto. Serve with parmesan cheese if desired. Serves 4.

penne with wilted rocket and prosciutto

simple cream pasta with lemon and basil

simple cream pasta with lemon and basil

400g (14 oz) tagliatelle or spaghetti
1 cup (8 fl oz) (single or pouring) cream
2 teaspoons finely grated lemon rind
2 tablespoons lemon juice
½ cup finely grated parmesan cheese
½ cup roughly chopped basil leaves
cracked black pepper
grated parmesan cheese to serve

Place the pasta in a large saucepan of salted boiling water and cook until al dente. Drain and return to the pan. Add the cream, lemon rind and juice, parmesan, basil and pepper. Toss to combine. Place in bowls and serve with parmesan. Serves 4.

VARIATIONS

+ **chicken** Toss 2 cups cooked shredded chicken and ½ cup toasted pine nuts through the pasta before serving.

+ **spinach and smoked salmon** Stir 100g (3½ oz) baby spinach leaves and 100g (3½ oz) chopped smoked salmon through the pasta before serving.

+ **prosciutto and egg** Omit the lemon rind. Replace the basil with flat-leaf parsley and stir through 3 egg yolks. Top with shreds of prosciutto* to serve.

pasta with caramelised onions

lime and coconut chicken rice

lemon and herb chicken pilaf

pasta with caramelised onions

1 tablespoon butter
1 tablespoon vegetable oil
4 brown onions, sliced
½ teaspoon chopped rosemary leaves
6 anchovy fillets, chopped
1 cup (8 fl oz) beef stock
1 cup black olives
400g (14 oz) spaghetti
parmesan cheese to serve

Place the butter, oil, onions and rosemary in a frying pan over medium heat. Cook, stirring occasionally, for 10 minutes or until the onions are golden and soft. Stir in the anchovies, stock and olives and cook for 1 minute or until slightly thickened. Cook the pasta in a large saucepan of salted boiling water until al dente. Drain and toss with the caramelised onions. Serve with the parmesan. Serves 4.

lime and coconut chicken rice

2 cups jasmine rice
2½ cups (20 fl oz) water
3 cups shredded cooked chicken
1 baby cos (romaine) lettuce, trimmed, leaves separated
dressing
¾ cup (6 fl oz) coconut cream
¾ cup (6 fl oz) lime juice
¼ cup (2 fl oz) fish sauce*
½ cup chopped mint
1 large red chilli, seeded and chopped

Place the rice and water in a saucepan over medium heat and cook until most of the liquid has been absorbed and tunnels have formed in the rice. Cover and set aside for 5 minutes. To make the dressing, combine the coconut cream, lime juice, fish sauce, mint and chilli. When the rice is cooked, toss with the dressing and chicken and place in a serving bowl lined with the cos lettuce leaves. Serves 4.

lemon and herb chicken pilaf

2 teaspoons vegetable oil
1 onion, chopped
2 teaspoons oregano leaves
sea salt and cracked black pepper
1 cup basmati* or long-grain rice
3 cups (24 fl oz) chicken stock
4 chicken breast fillets, cut into thirds
sea salt and cracked black pepper, extra
2 teaspoons vegetable oil, extra
¼ cup chopped flat-leaf parsley
100g (3½ oz) baby spinach leaves
1 tablespoon lemon zest

Heat a saucepan over medium-high heat. Add the oil, onion, oregano, salt and pepper and cook for 3 minutes or until the onion is soft. Add the rice and stock, bring to the boil, reduce the heat, cover with a tight-fitting lid and cook for 12 minutes or until the rice is al dente. While the rice is cooking, heat a frying pan over medium-high heat. Sprinkle the chicken with salt and pepper and add to the pan with the extra oil. Cook for 4 minutes each side or until the chicken is cooked through. To serve, stir the parsley, spinach and lemon zest through the rice and spoon onto serving plates. Top with the chicken and serve with a squeeze of lemon. Serves 4.

five-spice pork fried rice

2 teaspoons vegetable oil
1 teaspoon chinese five-spice powder*
1 tablespoon grated ginger
½ teaspoon chilli flakes
500g (1 lb) pork fillet, sliced
2 tablespoons vegetable oil, extra
6 cups cooked cold rice
4 green onions (scallions), sliced
200g (7 oz) snow peas (mange tout), shredded
2 tablespoons soy sauce
hoisin sauce* to serve

Heat a frying pan over high heat. Add the oil, five-spice, ginger and chilli and cook for 30 seconds. Add the pork and cook for 5 minutes or until well browned. Remove from the pan and set aside. Add the extra oil and rice and cook, stirring, for 5 minutes or until the rice is hot. Add the green onions and snow peas and cook for 2 minutes. Stir through the cooked pork and soy sauce. Serve in bowls with the hoisin sauce on the side. Serves 4.

five-spice pork fried rice

baked risotto with bacon and peas

1 tablespoon olive oil
2 rashers bacon, chopped
2 leeks, sliced
1 tablespoon thyme leaves
2 cups arborio rice*
5 cups (2 pints) chicken stock
1 cup frozen green peas
4 rashers bacon, extra
¾ cup grated parmesan cheese
2 tablespoons chopped mint
sea salt and cracked black pepper

Preheat the oven to 200°C (390°F). Heat a frying pan over high heat. Add the oil, bacon, leeks and thyme and cook for 5 minutes or until the leeks are lightly browned. Spoon the mixture into a 10 cup (4 pint) capacity ovenproof dish. Add the rice and stock and stir. Cover tightly with aluminium foil and bake for 30 minutes. Add the peas, re-cover and cook for a further 10 minutes. Place the extra bacon on a tray and cook in the oven for 8 minutes or until crisp. Remove the risotto from the oven, add the parmesan, mint, salt and pepper and stir for 4 minutes or until the risotto has thickened. To serve, place in bowls and crumble over the crispy bacon. Serves 4.

VARIATIONS

+ **pumpkin and fetta** Omit the bacon from the recipe. Add 300g (10 oz) peeled and chopped pumpkin to the dish with the cooked leeks, rice and stock. Replace the mint with basil and crumble 100g (3½ oz) fetta cheese over the top of the cooked risotto.

+ **asparagus and lemon** Omit the bacon from the recipe. Add 1 tablespoon grated lemon rind and 2 tablespoons lemon juice to the cooked leeks, rice and stock. At the same time as the peas, add 400g (14 oz) trimmed and halved asparagus.

+ **chicken and spinach** Omit the bacon from the recipe. Omit the peas and instead stir through 3 cups cooked shredded chicken, 50g (1½ oz) baby spinach leaves and 2 teaspoons grated lemon rind at the same time as the parmesan and mint.

baked risotto with bacon and peas

hokkien noodle stir-fry

2 teaspoons vegetable oil
½ cup (4 fl oz) sweet chilli sauce
2 tablespoons soy sauce
1 tablespoon fish sauce*
3 chicken breast fillets, sliced
400g (14 oz) broccolini or broccoli, halved or chopped
800g (1¾ lb) fresh hokkien noodles*
½ cup roasted unsalted cashew nuts

Heat a wok or deep frying pan over high heat. Add the oil, sweet chilli, soy and fish sauce and cook, stirring, for 4 minutes or until thick. Add the chicken and cook for 4 minutes or until cooked through. Add the broccolini or broccoli and cook for a further 3 minutes. Place the noodles in a bowl, cover with boiling water, stand for 2–4 minutes or until softened, stir to separate and drain. Add to the pan with the cashews and cook, stirring, for 1–2 minutes or until heated through. Serves 4.

pasta with herbs and greens

400g (14 oz) orecchiette or rigatoni
1 tablespoon butter
¾ cup (6 fl oz) chicken stock
200g (7 oz) broccoli, cut into small florets
100g (3½ oz) green beans, quartered
¾ cup green peas
80g (2½ oz) baby spinach leaves
sea salt and cracked black pepper
¼ cup shredded basil
¼ cup shredded mint

Cook the pasta in a large saucepan of salted boiling water until al dente. Drain. While the pasta is cooking, heat a frying pan over medium-high heat. Add the butter and stock and bring to a simmer. Add the broccoli, beans and peas, cover and cook for 2–3 minutes or until tender. Stir through the spinach, salt, pepper and cooked pasta. Sprinkle with the basil and mint and some grated parmesan cheese if desired. Serves 4.

hokkien noodle stir-fry

pasta with herbs and greens

spicy rice noodles

spicy rice noodles

400g (14 oz) fresh or dried thick rice noodles
2 tablespoons vegetable oil
2 teaspoons grated ginger
1 teaspoon mild chilli flakes
6 green onions (scallions), chopped
150g (5 oz) green beans, trimmed and halved
½ cup (4 fl oz) chicken stock
2 tablespoons lime juice
½ tablespoon brown sugar
1 tablespoon fish sauce*
⅔ cup (5 fl oz) oyster sauce*
½ cup coriander (cilantro) leaves
½ cup chopped roasted unsalted peanuts

Place the rice noodles in a bowl and cover with boiling water. Allow to stand for 2 minutes for fresh noodles or 5 minutes for dried, stir to separate, then drain. Heat a wok over high heat. Add the oil, ginger and chilli and cook for 2 minutes. Add the onions and beans and cook for 3 minutes. Add the chicken stock, lime juice, sugar, fish sauce, oyster sauce and rice noodles and cook, stirring, for 2 minutes. Toss through the coriander and peanuts and serve. Serves 4.

VARIATIONS

+ **chicken** Add 3 sliced chicken breast fillets when cooking the ginger and chilli and cook for a further 4 minutes or until the chicken is cooked through.

+ **egg** Whisk together 4 eggs and 1 teaspoon sesame oil. When the recipe is completed, pour the eggs into the wok, swirl around and cook for 1 minute. Remove from the wok, slice and serve on top of the noodles.

+ **pork** Add 600g (20 oz) trimmed and sliced pork fillet when cooking the ginger and chilli and cook for a further 4 minutes or until the pork is cooked through.

short cuts

the question of oil

Many people add oil to the pot when cooking spaghetti in the belief that this will stop it from sticking together. All it does, however, is float to the top and make the saucepan greasy. The only ingredient you need to add to the water is a good pinch of sea salt. Gently stirring the pasta once as it's cooking will separate the strands.

use your noodles

A variety of fresh noodles is available from specialty asian food stores and many supermarkets. They are easy and quick to prepare – just place in a bowl, cover with boiling water, stand until softened, stir to separate and drain. They're then ready to use in dishes such as stir-fries, soups and salads.

flash in the saucepan

If you are really keen on saving extra minutes in the kitchen, buy thinner or smaller pasta at the supermarket. Some varieties, such as spaghettini (the thin version of spaghetti), cook in as little as 4–5 minutes. Whatever thickness you choose, pasta should always only be cooked to al dente.

with the grain

Dishes such as fried rice and rice salad are better made with cold rice. Be prepared by putting on some extra rice next time you're cooking it and freezing the leftovers in 3 cup portions (or whatever seems sensible for your family's size). Remove from the freezer in the morning and it should be defrosted by dinner.

chicken

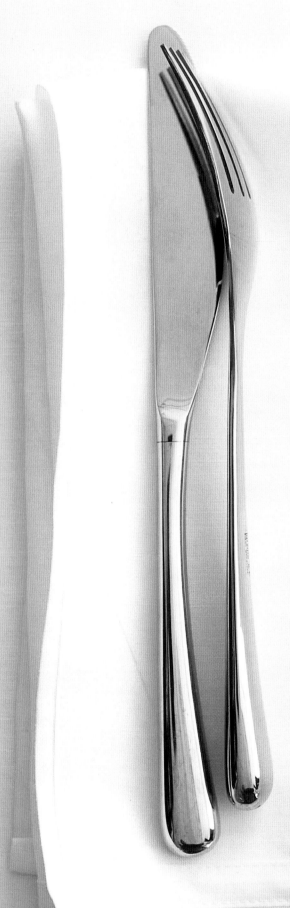

free range Is there anyone who can resist the juicy temptation of freshly cooked chicken? Golden roasted, sautéed to sticky perfection or simmered with spices, it can be served in so many ways, even when time is short. From a special lunch to a simple post-work supper, preparing chicken is the way to ensure everyone leaves a clean plate.

crispy chinese chicken

lemon and parsley chicken

soy chicken and rice pot

green olive baked chicken

crispy chinese chicken

4 chicken breast fillets
1½ teaspoons sea salt
2½ teaspoons chinese five-spice powder*
1 tablespoon peanut oil

Sprinkle both sides of the chicken with the combined salt and five-spice powder. Heat the oil in a frying pan over high heat. Place the chicken in the pan and cook for 4 minutes each side or until cooked through. Cut into pieces and serve with steamed snow peas (mange tout) tossed in hoisin sauce*. Serves 4.

lemon and parsley chicken

1 tablespoon olive oil
4 chicken breast fillets, halved lengthwise
cracked black pepper
1½ tablespoons olive oil, extra
2 tablespoons capers*
1 teaspoon chilli flakes
1 tablespoon finely grated lemon rind
2 cloves garlic, sliced
2 tablespoons lemon juice
½ cup chopped parsley

Heat the oil in a frying pan over medium heat. Sprinkle the chicken with the pepper and add to the pan. Cook for 5 minutes each side or until browned. Add the extra oil, capers, chilli, lemon rind and garlic, cook for 1 minute, then add the lemon juice and parsley. Serve with a rocket (arugula) salad. Serves 4.

soy chicken and rice pot

½ cup (4 fl oz) soy sauce
⅔ cup (5 fl oz) sherry or chinese cooking wine*
⅓ cup sugar
1 tablespoon grated ginger
4 chicken breast fillets
2 cups jasmine rice
3½ cups (28 fl oz) water
3 green onions (scallions), shredded

Place the soy, sherry or chinese wine, sugar and ginger in a frying pan over high heat and bring to the boil. Add the chicken and cook for 2 minutes each side. Place the rice and water into a deep frying pan over high heat. Cook for 4–5 minutes or until tunnels have formed in the rice and most of the water has been absorbed. Top with the chicken, cover and cook over very low heat for 5–6 minutes or until the chicken is cooked through. While the chicken is cooking, simmer the soy mixture for 2 minutes or until syrupy.
To serve, place the chicken and rice on plates, sprinkle with the green onions and spoon over the pan sauce. Serves 4.

green olive baked chicken

½ cup pitted green olives
¼ cup flat-leaf parsley
2 tablespoons lemon juice
cracked black pepper
4 chicken breast fillets

Preheat the oven to 200ºC (390ºF). Place the olives, parsley, lemon juice and pepper into a small food processor and process until roughly chopped. Line a baking dish with baking paper. Place the chicken in the dish and spread over the green olive paste. Bake for 20 minutes or until cooked through. Serve hot or cold with lemon wedges and a simple tomato and basil salad. Serves 4.

chicken roasted on eggplant and tomatoes

1 eggplant (aubergine), thickly sliced
3 roma tomatoes, sliced
1 tablespoon oregano leaves
sea salt and cracked black pepper
4 chicken breast fillets
½ cup grated parmesan cheese
½ cup grated mozzarella cheese

Preheat the oven to 180ºC (355ºF). Line a baking tray with baking paper. Place the eggplant slices on the tray and top with the tomatoes, oregano, salt and pepper. Top each pile with a chicken breast and sprinkle with the parmesan and mozzarella. Bake for 20 minutes or until the cheese is golden and the chicken cooked through. Serves 4.

chicken roasted on eggplant and tomatoes

grilled chicken and vegetable stacks

grilled chicken and vegetable stacks

4 chicken breast fillets, halved lengthwise
2 red capsicums (bell peppers), quartered
1 eggplant (aubergine), sliced lengthwise
2 small zucchinis (courgettes), sliced lengthwise
3 tablespoons olive oil
2 tablespoons lemon juice
sea salt and cracked black pepper
80g (3 oz) rocket (arugula) leaves
1 tablespoon store-bought pesto
½ cup whole-egg mayonnaise

Preheat a char-grill (broiler) or barbecue over high heat. Place the chicken, capsicums, eggplant, zucchinis, oil, lemon juice, salt and pepper in a bowl and toss to coat. Cook the chicken for 3–4 minutes on the grill or barbecue before adding the capsicums, eggplant and zucchinis and cooking until the chicken is golden and cooked through and the vegetables tender. To serve, place the chicken, vegetables and rocket in a stack on plates and serve topped with the combined pesto and mayonnaise. Serves 4.

VARIATIONS

+ **vegetable** Replace the chicken with 16 asparagus spears and grill with the vegetables. When stacking the vegetables add 4 sliced bocconcini*.

+ **beef with aioli** Replace the chicken breasts with 8 thin beef steaks. Replace the eggplant and capsicums with 2 thickly sliced tomatoes and 8 small field mushrooms. Replace the pesto with 1 clove crushed garlic.

+ **pork with apple** Replace the chicken breasts with 8 thin pork steaks. Add 2 cored and sliced apples to the vegetables. Replace the pesto and mayonnaise with 1½ tablespoons dijon mustard combined with ½ cup sour cream.

sticky thai chicken

baked italian chicken

parmesan crusted chicken

sticky thai chicken

2 teaspoons vegetable or peanut oil
4 large red chillies, seeded and chopped
1 tablespoon grated ginger
3 tablespoons lime juice
3 tablespoons fish sauce*
⅓ cup brown sugar
8 chicken thigh fillets, halved
2 tablespoons coriander (cilantro) leaves, optional

Heat a frying pan over medium-high heat. Add the oil, chillies and ginger and cook for 1 minute. Add the lime juice, fish sauce and brown sugar and cook, stirring, for 1 minute. Add the chicken and cook for 8 minutes. Increase the heat to high, turn the chicken and cook for a further 5 minutes or until golden, sticky and cooked through. Sprinkle with the coriander and serve with jasmine rice or steamed vegetables. Serves 4.

baked italian chicken

6 roma tomatoes, halved
3 teaspoons olive oil
sea salt and cracked black pepper
3 tablespoons store-bought pesto
4 chicken breast fillets
8 slices parmesan cheese
12 slices prosciutto*

Preheat the oven to 200°C (390°F). Place the tomatoes, cut side up, in a baking dish lined with baking paper, drizzle with the oil and sprinkle with the salt and pepper. Bake for 20 minutes. Spread the pesto over the chicken breasts, top with the parmesan and then wrap each in prosciutto. Place the chicken in the baking dish with the tomatoes and bake for 10–15 minutes or until the chicken is cooked through. Serve hot or cold with a simple green salad. Serves 4.

parmesan crusted chicken

4 chicken breast fillets
2 egg whites, lightly beaten
2 cups finely grated parmesan cheese⁺
cracked black pepper

Preheat the oven to 200°C (390°F). Line a baking tray with baking paper. Dip the chicken breasts into the egg whites, then toss in the combined parmesan and pepper to coat. Place in the baking tray and cook for 15 minutes or until the chicken is golden and cooked through. Serve with a simple rocket (arugula) and tomato salad. Serves 4.
⁺ You must use good quality parmesan for a crunchy crust.

simmered red curry chicken

2 teaspoons red curry paste*
400ml (12 fl oz) can coconut milk
1½ cups (12 fl oz) chicken stock
1 stalk lemongrass, crushed
4 chicken breast fillets
1 tablespoon lime juice
1 tablespoon brown sugar
1 tablespoon fish sauce*
⅓ cup coriander (cilantro) leaves

Heat a large deep non-stick frying pan over medium heat. Add the red curry paste and cook, stirring, for 1 minute. Add the coconut milk, stock and lemongrass and stir to combine. Bring to the boil and cook for 1 minute. Reduce the heat to low, add the chicken breasts and simmer for 10–12 minutes or until cooked through. Remove the lemongrass and discard. Remove the chicken breasts, set aside and keep warm. Stir the lime juice, sugar and fish sauce into the sauce and cook for a further 5 minutes or until slightly thickened. Serve the chicken with steamed greens and jasmine rice, and topped with the simmered coconut sauce and the coriander leaves. Serves 4.

simmered red curry chicken

quick flat roasted chicken

1.8kg (3½ lb) chicken
1 lemon, sliced
8 sprigs thyme
6 cloves garlic, unpeeled
olive oil for brushing
sea salt and cracked black pepper

Preheat the oven to 200°C (390°F). Using kitchen scissors, cut along the backbone of the chicken, then press firmly on the breastbone to flatten it. Place in a baking dish lined with baking paper. Add the lemon, thyme and garlic. Brush with the oil, then sprinkle with salt and pepper. Toss to combine. Bake for 35–45 minutes or until cooked through. Serve with a simple salad. Serves 4.

VARIATIONS

+ **soy and spice** Replace the lemon, thyme and garlic with 5 cinnamon sticks and 2 star anise*. Place under the chicken in the baking dish. Place 1 tablespoon soy sauce, ¼ cup (2 fl oz) water, 3 teaspoons brown sugar and ½ teaspoon chinese five-spice powder* into a small saucepan over medium heat and simmer for 1 minute. Brush over the chicken and bake.

+ **herb and pepper** Add 10 sprigs oregano and 5 sprigs tarragon to the basic recipe to be placed under the chicken. After brushing the chicken with the oil, add ¼ cup chopped oregano leaves, 1 tablespoon chopped tarragon and extra pepper to the basic sprinkling mixture.

+ **chilli and lime** Replace the lemon with a lime, and the thyme and garlic with 4 seeded and chopped large red chillies, 2 tablespoons finely grated lime rind, 1 tablespoon olive oil, 2 tablespoons lime juice and sea salt. Combine these ingredients, rub over both sides of the chicken and bake.

quick flat roasted chicken

jo's chinese-style chicken omelette

2 teaspoons sesame oil
1 teaspoon finely grated ginger
2 green onions (scallions), shredded
50g (1½ oz) snow peas (mange tout), trimmed and sliced
100g (3 oz) cooked and shredded chicken
4 eggs, lightly beaten
50g (1½ oz) beansprouts
hoisin or chilli sauce to serve

Heat a medium non-stick frying pan over medium heat. Add
the sesame oil, ginger, green onions and snow peas to the
pan and cook for 3 minutes or until the snow peas are tender.
Add the chicken to the pan and cook for 1 minute or until
heated. Pour over the eggs and stir once to distribute. Cook
over low heat for 5 minutes or until the eggs are set. Fold the
omelette in half, place on a serving plate and top with the
beansprouts. Serve with hoisin or chilli sauce. Serves 2.

simmered tomato and basil chicken

1 tablespoon olive oil
1 onion, sliced
2 cloves garlic, sliced
4 chicken breast fillets
500ml (15 fl oz) tomato puree
¼ cup (2 fl oz) white wine
1 teaspoon sugar
½ cup roughly chopped basil leaves
½ cup black olives
shaved parmesan cheese to serve

Heat the oil in a frying pan over high heat. Add the onion and
garlic and cook for 2 minutes or until soft. Add the chicken
and cook for 2 minutes each side or until well browned. Add
the tomato puree, wine and sugar and simmer over medium
heat for 8 minutes or until the chicken is cooked through. Stir
through the basil and olives. To serve, place the chicken on
plates and top with the pan sauce. Serve with steamed greens
and the shaved parmesan. Serves 4.

jo's chinese-style chicken omelette

simmered tomato and basil chicken

thai lime and lemongrass chicken

thai lime and lemongrass chicken

2 teaspoons vegetable oil
1 tablespoon grated ginger
1 stalk lemongrass, finely chopped
1 teaspoon chilli flakes
650g (21 oz) chicken mince
¼ cup (2 fl oz) lime juice
¼ cup (2 fl oz) fish sauce*
1 tablespoon sugar
¾ cup coriander (cilantro) leaves
¾ cup basil leaves
4 green onions (scallions), shredded
rice noodles to serve

Heat a frying pan over high heat. Add the oil, ginger, lemongrass and chilli and cook for 1 minute. Add the chicken mince and cook, stirring, for 6–7 minutes or until cooked through. Stir through the lime juice, fish sauce, sugar, coriander, basil and green onions. Serve with hot rice noodles or salad leaves. Serves 4.

VARIATIONS

+ **pork with lime and peanuts** Replace the chicken mince with pork mince. Stir ⅓ cup chopped roasted unsalted peanuts and 150g (5 oz) mizuna* leaves into the finished dish.

+ **prawns with lime and lemongrass** Replace the chicken mince with 550g (18½ oz) roughly chopped peeled green (raw) prawns (shrimp), add an extra tablespoon lime juice and serve on cos (romaine) lettuce leaves.

+ **beef with lime and tomato** Replace the chicken mince with beef mince. Stir 2 chopped tomatoes into the finished dish.

short cuts

a snip in time

To reduce the time it takes to roast or grill (broil) a whole chicken, flatten it out. Take a sharp pair of kitchen scissors, cut along the backbone of the chicken, then press firmly on the breastbone to flatten it. This method also allows you to flavour both the inside and outside of a bird with relative ease.

breast by far

Chicken breasts can be tricky to prepare; if you sear them over heat until they're cooked through the outside can end up over-brown and tough. To cook breasts perfectly, brown them over high heat on both sides, then drop the temperature right down, put the lid on the pan and leave them to cook slowly.

half measures

Another way to reduce cooking time is to butterfly whole chicken breasts. Take a sharp knife and carefully cut them lengthwise but not all the way through. When folded out, the butterflied breasts will resemble a heart shape that's great for pan-frying, grilling (broiling) and barbecuing.

ready to go

Barbecued chicken is the ultimate convenience food. For fast dinners, serve it still warm with a simple salad or piled high on fresh white bread with lettuce and mayonnaise. Any leftover meat can be stripped off the bone and added to quicker-than-ever stir-fries, pasta dishes, asian-style noodles or soups.

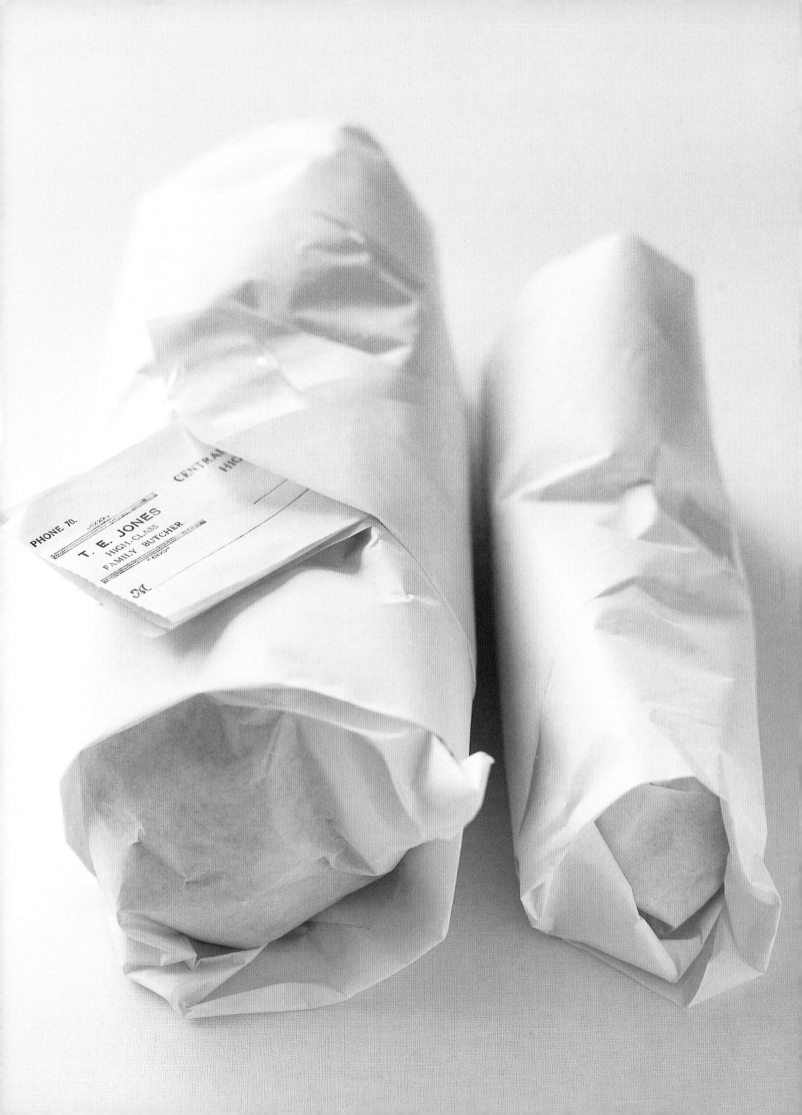

PHONE 70.

T. E. JONES
HIGH-CLASS
FAMILY BUTCHER

CENTRAL

meat

flash in the pan
There's nothing that says welcome home like the aroma of a lamb roast baking in the oven or the sound of steaks sizzling in a pan. And, contrary to popular opinion, you don't need hours to bring these – and other – favourite dishes to the table. A spicy stir-fry in 10 minutes? Lamb pie in half an hour? It's simpler than you think.

lamb baked on figs and fennel

lamb cutlets with grilled goat's cheese

wrapped and roasted beef fillet

oregano veal chops with white bean salad

lamb baked on figs and fennel

4 baby or small fennel bulbs, sliced
6 figs, halved
2 tablespoons olive oil
sea salt and cracked black pepper
¼ cup (2 fl oz) white wine vinegar
2 tablespoons brown sugar
2 x 6-cutlet lamb racks, trimmed

Preheat the oven to 200°C (390°F). Line a baking tray with baking paper. Place the fennel and figs on the tray. Combine the oil, salt, pepper, vinegar and sugar, pour over the fennel and figs and bake for 10 minutes. Sprinkle the lamb with salt and pepper and add to the pan. Cook for a further 20 minutes or until the lamb is cooked to your liking. To serve, place the fennel mixture on serving plates, slice the lamb into cutlets, place on the fennel, then spoon over the pan juices. Serves 4.

lamb cutlets with grilled goat's cheese

8–10 lamb cutlets, trimmed
2 tablespoons lemon juice
1 tablespoon olive oil
sea salt and cracked black pepper
2 tablespoons oregano or marjoram leaves
8–10 thin slices goat's cheese
lemon wedges to serve

Place the lamb cutlets in a dish with the combined lemon juice, oil, salt and pepper and set aside for 5–10 minutes. Place the cutlets under a preheated hot grill (broiler) and cook for 1–2 minutes on one side. Turn the cutlets and cook for 1 minute. Sprinkle with the oregano or marjoram and top each cutlet with a slice of the goat's cheese. Grill for 3 minutes or until the cheese is golden. Serve with the lemon wedges and steamed greens or a simple salad. Serves 4.

wrapped and roasted beef fillet

650g (21 oz) eye fillet
2 tablespoons horseradish cream*
cracked black pepper
8–12 slices prosciutto*

Preheat the oven to 190°C (375°F). Trim the fillet of any sinew. Spread the horseradish over the beef and sprinkle with the pepper. Wrap the prosciutto around the beef, tucking all the ends under the fillet. Place in a baking tray lined with baking paper and cook for 25 minutes (rare), 35 minutes (medium) or 45 minutes (well done). To serve, slice and serve with roast vegetables. Serves 4.

oregano veal chops with white bean salad

30g (1 oz) butter
1 tablespoon lemon juice
1 tablespoon oregano leaves
cracked black pepper
8 small veal chops or 4 veal t-bone steaks
lemon wedges to serve
white bean salad
400g (14 oz) can white beans*, drained and rinsed
2 large tomatoes, chopped
100g (3½ oz) baby rocket (arugula) leaves
½ red onion, chopped
¼ cup (2 fl oz) lemon juice
2 tablespoons olive oil
sea salt and cracked black pepper

Heat a frying pan over high heat. Add the butter, lemon juice, oregano and pepper to the pan and cook for 1 minute. Add the veal and cook for 4–5 minutes each side or until cooked to your liking. While the veal is cooking make the white bean salad by combining the white beans, tomatoes, rocket, onion, lemon juice, oil, salt and pepper and tossing lightly.
To serve, place the white bean salad on plates, top with the veal and place lemon wedges on the side. Serves 4.

caramelised soy pork

1 teaspoon sesame oil
1 tablespoon finely grated ginger
½ teaspoon chilli flakes
⅓ cup (2½ fl oz) soy sauce
½ cup (4 fl oz) honey
¼ cup (2 fl oz) dry sherry
2 x 250g (8 oz) pork fillets, trimmed

Place the sesame oil, ginger and chilli in a frying pan over high heat and cook for 1 minute. Add the soy, honey and sherry and cook, stirring, for 2 minutes. Cut each pork fillet in half and add to the pan. Cook in the pan sauce for 10–15 minutes each side or until cooked to your liking. Serve with shredded chilli, steamed rice and greens. Serves 4.

caramelised soy pork

veal cutlets with tomato pan sauce

veal cutlets with tomato pan sauce

8 veal cutlets
2 teaspoons oil
sea salt and cracked black pepper
baby spinach leaves to serve
tomato pan sauce
1 tablespoon butter
1 tablespoon olive oil
250g (8 oz) cherry tomatoes, halved
250g (8 oz) yellow pear tomatoes, halved
1 teaspoon sugar
½ cup roughly chopped basil leaves
sea salt and cracked black pepper

Brush the cutlets with the oil, then sprinkle with salt and pepper. Heat a non-stick frying pan over high heat. Add the cutlets to the pan and cook for 3–4 minutes each side or until cooked to your liking. Place the cutlets on a warm plate, cover and set aside.

For the tomato pan sauce, place the butter and oil in the pan and heat until the butter is bubbling. Add the tomatoes and cook for 3 minutes or until just beginning to soften. Stir through the sugar, basil, salt and pepper. To serve, place the spinach leaves on plates, top with the cutlets and spoon over the pan sauce. Serves 4.

VARIATIONS

+ **chicken and fetta** Replace the veal cutlets with 4 chicken breast fillets. For the sauce, add 1 tablespoon capers and replace the basil with 1 tablespoon flat-leaf parsley. To serve, top the chicken and tomato sauce with crumbled fetta cheese.

+ **beef and balsamic** Replace the veal cutlets with 4 x 250g (8 oz) sirloin steaks. For the sauce, replace the basil with 1 tablespoon thyme leaves and add 1 tablespoon balsamic vinegar. Serve on steamed asparagus and green beans.

+ **haloumi and fennel** Replace the veal cutlets with 500g (1 lb) sliced haloumi cheese cooked for 1 minute each side, and 2 sliced fennel bulbs cooked for 2 minutes each side in 1 tablespoon oil. Add ½ cup black olives to the tomato sauce and serve with rocket (arugula).

roast veal, potato, zucchini and eggplant

pan-fried spinach and mozzarella veal

steak with rocket sauce

roast veal, potato, zucchini and eggplant

1 x 6–8 cutlet veal rack
8 kipfler potatoes, sliced
½ cup (4 fl oz) white wine
4 zucchinis (courgettes), halved
2 small eggplants (aubergines), sliced
1 tablespoon olive oil
2 tablespoons oregano leaves
sea salt and cracked black pepper
mustard sour cream dressing
1 tablespoon wholegrain mustard
½ cup sour cream

Preheat the oven to 220ºC (425ºF). Trim the veal rack.
Heat a frying pan over high heat. Add the rack and cook for
2 minutes on each side or until browned. Set aside. Place
the potatoes and half the wine in a baking dish lined with
baking paper. Roast for 10 minutes. Place the zucchinis
and eggplants in a bowl with the olive oil, oregano, salt and
pepper and toss well to coat. Add to the baking dish with the
remaining wine, top with the veal rack and roast for a further
25–30 minutes or until cooked to your liking.
For the dressing, combine the mustard and sour cream. To
serve, slice the veal rack into cutlets, spoon over the dressing
and serve with the potatoes, zucchini and eggplant. Serves 4.

pan-fried spinach and mozzarella veal

4 x 150g (5 oz) thin schnitzel-style veal steaks
150g (5 oz) baby spinach leaves
8 small slices mozzarella cheese
olive oil for brushing
sea salt and cracked black pepper

Pound the veal steaks until 3–4mm (⅛ in–⅙ in) thick. Place
the spinach leaves in a heatproof bowl, cover with boiling
water and stand for 30 seconds before draining very well.
Place the spinach and mozzarella on one half of each veal
steak and fold over the veal to enclose. Press the edges to
roughly seal. Brush the veal with a little olive oil and sprinkle
with salt and pepper. Cook the veal in a hot non-stick frying
pan for 2–3 minutes each side or until cooked to your liking.
Serve with a simple salad. Serves 4.

steak with rocket sauce

4 x 180g (6 oz) steaks
oil for brushing
sea salt and cracked black pepper
40g (1½ oz) butter
1½ tablespoons lemon juice
2 teaspoons sugar
2 cloves garlic, crushed
200g (7 oz) baby rocket (arugula) leaves, trimmed

Brush the steaks with a little oil and sprinkle with the salt and
pepper. Heat a non-stick frying pan over high heat. Add the
steak and cook for 3–4 minutes each side or until cooked to
your liking. Place the steaks on warm serving plates, cover
and rest. Add the butter, lemon juice and sugar to the hot pan
and cook, stirring, for 1 minute. Add the garlic and rocket and
toss until the rocket has just wilted. Place on the steaks and
serve. Serves 4.

ginger pork stir-fry

1 teaspoon sesame oil
1 teaspoon vegetable oil
1 clove garlic, crushed
2 tablespoons shredded ginger
2 brown onions, cut into wedges
2 x 350g (12 oz) pork fillets, sliced
¼ cup (2 fl oz) oyster sauce
¼ cup (2 fl oz) chicken stock
300g (10 oz) baby spinach leaves

Heat a large frying pan or wok over high heat. Add the oils,
garlic, ginger and onions and stir-fry for 3 minutes. Add the
pork in batches and stir-fry for 4 minutes each or until well
browned. Returned the cooked pork to the pan, add the oyster
sauce and stock and cook for a further 2 minutes. Add the
spinach and stir for 1 minute or until just wilted. Serve with
rice or noodles. Serves 4.

ginger pork stir-fry

simple beef pies

4 x 125g (4 oz) fillet steaks
1 teaspoon oil
sea salt and cracked black pepper
2 x 375g (13 oz) packets store-bought puff pastry
2 tablespoons wholegrain mustard
1 egg, lightly beaten

Preheat the oven to 200°C (390°F). Trim the steaks, brush with the oil and sprinkle with salt and pepper. Heat a frying pan over high heat. Add the steaks and cook for 3 minutes each side or until well browned. Remove from the pan. Roll out the pastry on a lightly floured surface until 3mm (⅛ in) thick. Cut 4 x 14cm (5½ in) rounds for the base and 4 x 16cm (6 in) rounds for the tops.
Line a tray with baking paper and place the 4 pastry bases on the tray. Top each with a piece of beef and ½ tablespoon mustard. Brush the pastry edges with the egg and top with the remaining rounds of pastry. Press the edges to seal and brush the pastry top with the egg. Bake for 20 minutes or until the pastry is golden and the beef is cooked. Serve with a tomato chutney. Serves 4.

VARIATIONS

+ **chicken pies** Replace the beef steaks with 2 large chicken breasts. Follow the above recipe, cutting the cooked chicken breasts in half. Replace the grain mustard with 2 teaspoons dijon mustard, 2 tablespoons grated cheddar and 2 tablespoons parmesan cheese for each pie.

+ **pork pies** Replace the beef steaks with 2 x 300g (10 oz) pork fillets, trimmed and cut in half. Follow the above recipe, replacing the grain mustard with 1 tablespoon apple sauce and 1 teaspoon english mustard for each pie.

+ **lamb pies** Bring ¼ cup mint jelly to the boil in a small saucepan. Simmer for 2 minutes, then allow to cool. Replace the beef steaks with 2 x 250g (8 oz) lamb backstraps, trimmed and cut in half. Follow the above recipe, replacing the grain mustard with 1 tablespoon cooked mint jelly for each pie.

simple beef pies

honey mustard beef stir-fry

lamb fillets with apple mint salsa

steak with mushrooms and balsamic glaze

honey mustard beef stir-fry

650g (21 oz) rump or topside steak
2 teaspoons vegetable oil
1 clove garlic, crushed
2 onions, cut into wedges
⅓ cup dijon mustard
¼ cup (2 fl oz) honey
250g (8 oz) green vegetables, such as beans, snow peas
   (mange tout) or asparagus

Trim the steak and cut into slices. Heat a deep frying pan
or wok over high heat until very hot. Add the oil, garlic and
onions and cook for 2 minutes. Add the beef strips and cook
for 4 minutes or until well browned. Add the mustard,
honey and vegetables and toss to coat. Cook for a further
2–3 minutes or until the vegetables are just tender. Serve
with steamed rice. Serves 4.

lamb fillets with apple mint salsa

1 tablespoon vegetable oil
½ teaspoon mild chilli flakes
1 teaspoon ground cumin
sea salt and cracked black pepper
700g (23 oz) lamb fillets, trimmed
mint salsa
2 green apples, cores removed
1 cup mint leaves
2 tablespoons white wine vinegar
1 tablespoon honey

Combine the oil, chilli, cumin, salt and pepper in a shallow
dish. Add the lamb and toss to coat. Set aside while making
the mint salsa.
For the mint salsa, place the apples, mint, vinegar and honey
into a food processor and process until roughly chopped.
Cook the lamb on a preheated barbecue or in a hot frying
pan for 2–3 minutes each side or until cooked to your liking.
Slice the lamb and serve with the mint salsa and steamed
greens or a simple green salad. Serves 4.

steak with mushrooms and balsamic glaze

4 x 180g (6 oz) thick sirloin or fillet steaks
oil for brushing
sea salt and cracked black pepper
2 teaspoons olive oil
20 button mushrooms
20 small swiss brown mushrooms
2 tablespoons balsamic vinegar
3 teaspoons brown sugar
1½ cups (12 fl oz) beef stock
1 tablespoon tarragon leaves
¾ cup (6 fl oz) cream

Brush the steaks with a little oil and sprinkle well with salt
and pepper. Heat a frying pan over high heat. Add the steaks
and cook for 4 minutes each side or until cooked to your
liking. Place the steaks on a warm plate, cover and rest.
Add the olive oil and mushrooms to the pan and cook for
5 minutes. Set aside. Add the balsamic vinegar, sugar and
stock to the pan and boil for 8–10 minutes or until reduced.
Stir through the tarragon, cream and cooked mushrooms.
Season with salt.
To serve, place the steaks on plates and spoon over the
mushrooms and glaze. Serve with steamed vegetables,
roast potatoes or a simple salad. Serves 4.

marmalade glazed pork steaks

4 x 200g (7 oz) pork butterfly steaks
2 teaspoons vegetable oil
sea salt and cracked black pepper
1 tablespoon sage leaves
⅓ cup breakfast orange marmalade

Heat a frying pan over high heat. Brush the pork with oil and
sprinkle with salt and pepper. Add the pork and sage to the
pan and cook for 2 minutes each side or until well browned.
Add the marmalade to the pan and cook for a further
2 minutes each side or until cooked to your liking. Serve the
pork on steamed greens and spoon over the glaze. Serves 4.

marmalade glazed pork steaks

chilli jam beef stir-fry

chilli jam beef stir-fry

6 large mild red chillies, seeds removed
1 tablespoon roughly chopped ginger
1 onion, quartered
3 teaspoons shrimp paste*
⅓ cup brown sugar
2 tablespoons vegetable oil
650g (21 oz) beef strips
4 green onions (scallions), sliced
200g (7 oz) green beans, trimmed

Place the chillies, ginger, onion, shrimp paste, sugar and oil into a food processor and process until finely chopped. Heat a non-stick frying pan over medium-high heat and add the chilli paste. Cook, stirring, for 5–7 minutes or until the mixture is thick and fragrant. Add the beef to the pan and stir-fry for 3 minutes. Add the green onions and beans, cover and cook for a further 3 minutes or until the vegetables are tender. Serve with steamed jasmine rice. Serves 4.

VARIATIONS

+ **pork and basil** Follow the above recipe, replacing the beef with 2 x 300g (10 oz) pork fillets cut into strips and the beans with 200g (7 oz) snow peas (mange tout). Stir 1 cup beansprouts and ½ cup basil leaves into the finished dish.

+ **chicken and peanut** Follow the above recipe, replacing the beef with 6 chicken thigh fillets cut into strips. Stir ¼ cup chopped roasted unsalted peanuts and ½ cup coriander (cilantro) leaves into the finished dish. Serve with a squeeze of lime.

+ **mixed vegetables** Follow the above recipe, omitting the beef. When adding the beans and green onions, also add 4 quartered bok choy*, 2 cups halved button mushrooms and 200g (7 oz) chopped broccoli. Stir ⅓ cup chopped roasted unsalted cashew nuts into the finished dish.

short cuts

easy flavour

It is easy to serve condiments alongside cooked meats, but by spreading both sides of a steak, fillet or cutlet with its normal accompaniment before pan-frying or barbecuing you create a flavour-filled crust. Experiment with a variety of mustards, chutneys, horseradish, marmalades and mint jellies.

fast freeze

Buying extra meat and storing it in the freezer is an easy way of assuring there's always something for dinner. Before freezing, layer the steaks or other cuts with pieces of baking paper in between. This way, any number of steaks can be removed from the freezer and thawed without defrosting the whole lot.

use your butcher

Trimming sinew from meat, cleaning up racks of lamb or veal, and slicing up steaks ready for stir-frying are tasks your butcher is trained to do. By asking him to do these things for you, you know the job will be done well and finished in about a quarter of the time that it would take you to do it once you got home.

cooking perfection

If your family or guests like their steaks cooked to differing degrees, make the job easier by cutting a whole fillet into varying thicknesses: thin pieces for well done, medium for medium cook, and thick for rare. This way, whether you're pan-frying or barbecuing, all the steaks will be ready at once.

seafood

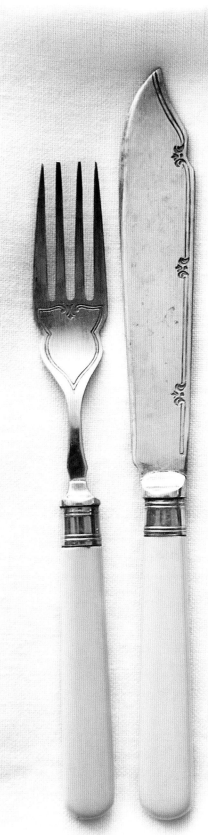

cast your net
There is a perception that all things fishy are simply too hard to contemplate preparing at home. Nothing could be further from the truth. Whether you love it straight up with just a squeeze of lemon or are looking for something that is a little more sophisticated, for fast, fresh meals seafood is hard to beat.

nori-wrapped salmon with wasabi mash

fish seared in dill and lemon

baked fish and chips

crispy fried fish with soy and ginger

nori-wrapped salmon with wasabi mash

4 x 180g (6 oz) salmon fillets
cracked black pepper
1 sheet nori*, quartered
1 tablespoon vegetable oil
80g (2½ oz) butter, melted
wasabi mash
1kg (2 lb) boiling potatoes, peeled and chopped
30g (1 oz) butter
1 tablespoon wasabi paste*
½ cup sour cream
2–3 tablespoons milk
sea salt

To make the mash, place the potatoes in a saucepan of cold salted water and bring to the boil. Cook until tender when tested with a skewer. Drain and return to the warm pan. Add the butter, wasabi, sour cream and milk and mash until smooth. Stir through the salt, cover and keep warm. To cook the salmon, sprinkle each fillet with pepper and wrap in a piece of nori. Heat a frying pan over high heat. Add the oil and salmon and cook, skin side down, for 3 minutes. Turn and cook for a further minute or until just cooked through. To serve, place the mash on plates, top with the salmon fillets and spoon over the melted butter. Serve with lemon wedges and steamed green vegetables. Serves 4.

fish seared in dill and lemon

½ cup dill leaves
½ cup flat-leaf parsley
2 tablespoons capers*
2 tablespoons dijon mustard
2 tablespoons lemon juice
2 tablespoons olive oil
sea salt and cracked black pepper
800g (¾ lb) firm white fish fillets, skin removed
1 tablespoon olive oil, extra

Place the dill, parsley, capers, mustard, lemon juice, oil, salt and pepper into a food processor and process until finely chopped. Cut the fish into large pieces and coat with the dill mixture. Heat a non-stick frying pan over high heat. Add the extra oil and the fish, a few pieces at a time, and cook for 2–3 minutes on each side or until the fish is well seared and just cooked through. Serve with a potato salad dressed with rocket (arugula) leaves, lemon juice and olive oil. Serves 4.

baked fish and chips

1kg (2 lb) desiree potatoes, thinly sliced
1 tablespoon vegetable oil
sea salt
4 x 200g (7 oz) firm white fish fillets
1 teaspoon finely grated lemon rind
sea salt and cracked black pepper

Preheat the oven to 220°C (425°F). Place a baking tray in the oven for 10 minutes to heat. Place the potatoes on a piece of baking paper. Place on the hot tray and sprinkle with the oil and salt and bake for 20 minutes. Sprinkle the fish with the lemon rind, salt and pepper, add to the tray and cook for 10 minutes or until the fish is just cooked through. Serves 4.

crispy fried fish with soy and ginger

20g (½ oz) shredded ginger
⅔ cup (5 fl oz) soy sauce
2 tablespoons lime juice
2 tablespoons brown sugar
4 x 400g (14 oz) small whole snapper, scaled and gutted
rice flour* for dusting
vegetable oil for shallow frying
4 green onions (scallions), sliced

For the sauce, place the ginger, soy, lime juice and brown sugar in a frying pan over high heat and cook for 2 minutes or until slightly reduced. Set aside.
Wash the fish, pat dry and score twice on each side. Dust with the rice flour and shake off any excess. Heat a large frying pan over high heat and add 5cm of oil. When the oil is hot add the fish, one at a time, and cook for 5 minutes each side or until crisp. Place in a warm oven while cooking the remaining fish. To serve, place the fish on plates, spoon over the sauce and top with the green onions. Serves 4.

chilli salt and pepper stir-fried squid

8 large squid hoods (600g/20 oz), rinsed and scored*
3 tablespoons vegetable oil
8 large mild chillies, seeded and sliced
1 tablespoon flaked sea salt
1 teaspoon roughly cracked black pepper
1 teaspoon chinese five-spice powder*

Cut the squid hoods into eighths. Combine the oil, chillies, salt, pepper and five-spice powder. Heat a frying pan over high heat. Add half the chilli mixture and cook for 1 minute. Add half the squid pieces and cook for 2–3 minutes or until the squid turns opaque and just cooked through. Remove from the pan and continue cooking with the remaining ingredients. Serve with steamed greens and lemon wedges. Serves 4.

chilli salt and pepper stir-fried squid

chilli and basil stir-fried prawns

chilli and basil stir-fried prawns

1 tablespoon vegetable oil
4 large red chillies, seeded and sliced
2 teaspoons grated ginger
1kg (2 lb) peeled green (raw) prawns (shrimp), tails intact
2 tablespoons fish sauce*
1 tablespoon brown sugar
2 tablespoons lime or lemon juice
1 cup small basil leaves

Heat a frying pan or wok over high heat. Add the oil, chillies and ginger and cook for 1 minute. Add the prawns and cook for 1 minute or until sealed. Combine the fish sauce, sugar and lime or lemon juice and pour over the prawns. Cook, stirring, for 3 minutes or until the prawns are just cooked through. Stir through the basil and serve with steamed greens and rice. Serves 4.

VARIATIONS

+ **chilli and basil fish** Replace the prawns with 750g (1½ lb) cubed firm white fish fillets. Add 50g (1½ oz) baby spinach leaves with the basil.

+ **chilli and coriander mussels** Replace the prawns with 1kg (2 lb) cleaned mussels and the basil with coriander (cilantro) leaves.

+ **chilli and mint squid** Replace the prawns with 8 small halved squid hoods (600g/20 oz) and the basil with mint leaves.

chilli and tomato fish

blackened spiced fish with cucumber salad

crunchy herb roasted fish

chilli and tomato fish

1 tablespoon olive oil
1 onion, sliced
¼ teaspoon chilli flakes
4 x 180g (6 oz) firm white fish fillets
sea salt and cracked black pepper
3 ripe tomatoes, cut into thin wedges
2 teaspoons grated lemon rind
2 tablespoons chopped flat-leaf parsley

Heat a frying pan over medium-high heat. Add the oil, onion and chilli and cook for 3 minutes. Sprinkle the fish with salt and pepper and add to the pan. Cook for 4–5 minutes each side or until just cooked through. Set aside and keep warm. Increase the heat to high, add the tomatoes and lemon rind to the pan and cook for 3 minutes or until just soft. Stir through the parsley. Place the fish on serving plates and top with the tomato sauce. Serves 4.

blackened spiced fish with cucumber salad

1 teaspoon sweet paprika
½ teaspoon chilli powder
1 teaspoon ground oregano
1 teaspoon ground cumin
½ teaspoon cracked black pepper
½ teaspoon sea salt
4 x 200g (7 oz) portions firm white fish
vegetable oil for brushing
cucumber salad
3 small cucumbers, thickly sliced
¾ cup roughly chopped mint leaves
2 green onions (scallions), sliced
¼ cup thick plain yoghurt
1 tablespoon lemon juice

Combine the paprika, chilli, oregano, cumin, pepper and salt. Brush the fish with oil and sprinkle generously with the spices. Heat a non-stick frying pan over high heat. Add the fish and cook for 6–8 minutes each side or until blackened. While the fish is cooking prepare the salad by combining the cucumbers, mint and onions. Combine the yoghurt and lemon juice, pour over the cucumbers and toss lightly to combine. Place on serving plates and top with the fish. Serves 4.

crunchy herb roasted fish

4 firm white fish fillets
herb topping
2 cups fresh breadcrumbs
2 teaspoons finely grated lemon zest
1 red chilli, seeded and chopped
2 tablespoons chopped flat-leaf parsley
2 tablespoons chopped dill
60g (2 oz) butter, melted
sea salt and cracked black pepper

Preheat the oven to 200°C (390°F). To make the herb topping, combine the breadcrumbs, lemon, chilli, parsley, dill, butter, salt and pepper. Place the fish fillets on a tray lined with baking paper. Press the herb topping over the fish. Bake for 12–15 minutes or until the fish is just cooked through and the herb topping is crisp. Serve with lemon wedges and a simple green salad. Serves 4.

crispy skin fish with lemon salsa

8 x 180g (6 oz) snapper, salmon or ocean trout fillets
vegetable oil for brushing
sea salt and cracked black pepper
lemon salsa
2 lemons, peeled and sliced
1½ tablespoons caster (superfine) sugar
½ cup roughly chopped flat-leaf parsley
2 tablespoons salted capers*, rinsed
sea salt and cracked black pepper

To make the lemon salsa, combine the lemons, sugar, parsley, capers, salt and pepper and set aside.
Brush the skin of the fish with the oil and sprinkle both sides with a little salt and pepper. Heat a non-stick frying pan over high heat. Add the fish to the pan, skin side down, and cook for 4 minutes or until the skin is crisp. Turn and cook for a further minute or until the fish is just cooked through.
To serve, place the fish on plates and top with the lemon salsa. Serve with a simple green salad. Serves 4.

crispy skin fish with lemon salsa

caramelised lime fish

1kg (2 lb) firm white fish fillets, skin removed
2 teaspoons vegetable oil
2 tablespoons lime juice
3 tablespoons brown sugar
1 teaspoon fish sauce*
1 tablespoon soy sauce
1 teaspoon chilli flakes
3 small cucumbers, sliced into ribbons
½ cup coriander (cilantro) leaves
4 green onions (scallions), sliced

Cut the fish into large pieces. Heat a non-stick frying pan over high heat. Add the oil and fish and cook for 1 minute on each side or until brown and sealed. Combine the lime juice, sugar, fish sauce, soy and chilli, add to the pan and cook, turning the fish once, for 4 minutes or until the fish is just cooked through and the sauce has reduced and is sticky. To serve, place the cucumbers, coriander and onions on plates and top with the fish. Spoon over the pan sauce and serve. Serves 4.

VARIATIONS

+ **caramelised lime scallops** Replace the fish with 16 scallops. Cook the sauce first for 4 minutes, then add the scallops and cook for 1 minute each side. Replace the cucumber salad with 2 sliced celery sticks, 1 cup mint leaves and 4 sliced green onions (scallions).

+ **caramelised lime salmon** Replace the white fish with 4 x 200g (7 oz) skinless salmon fillets, cooking for 2 minutes each side before adding the sauce to the pan. Replace the cucumber salad with 400g (14 oz) trimmed blanched asparagus and the leaves of a baby cos (romaine) lettuce.

+ **caramelised lime prawns** Replace the fish with 32 green (raw) shelled prawns (shrimp). Replace the cucumber salad with 100g (3½ oz) baby rocket (arugula) leaves and 2 small sliced avocados.

caramelised lime fish

short cuts

get fresh

To be sure you're eating the freshest fish possible, buy them whole. That way you get to check out the eyes, the simplest indicator of freshness – look for ones that are bright, not cloudy. Once you've made a selection, ask your fishmonger to do the filleting. The head and bones can be used for stock, if you have time.

waste time

Discarding prawn shells and other seafood leftovers can be a problem – put them out in the bin and you'll soon have an awful smell wafting around your home. Place any seafood scraps in layers of plastic bags, then wrap in newspaper and freeze. Only put them out in the bin the night before garbage collection.

frozen assets

Sometimes a whole fish can be too much for one meal, so cut the remaining fillets into portions and freeze in two- or four-person serves to use at a later time. Place baking paper between each portion and freeze in an airtight container, not just a plastic bag, to protect the delicate flesh from freezer burn.

head start

To take the hard work out of preparation and save yourself some time, order your seafood ahead and ask the fishmonger to ready it for cooking. He or she can clean squid hoods, baby octopus and mussels, peel green or cooked prawns and shuck fresh oysters for you provided you give enough notice.

vegetables

pick of the crop
They are the staple of any meal but have the potential to become – well, let's be honest – boring. With a dash of inspiration, however, the humble vege becomes supper star. The aniseed crunch of fennel, the soothing familiarity of potato, a ripe red tomato… These fresh offerings are not just side shows, they're the main event.

spicy roast vegetables with hummus

asparagus and potatoes with lemon butter

honey roast vegetables on pepper polenta

root vegetable fritters

spicy roast vegetables with hummus

750g (1½ lb) pumpkin, cut into wedges
1 orange sweet potato (kumara) (500g/1 lb), quartered
4 zucchinis (courgettes), halved
1 teaspoon sweet paprika
1 teaspoon ground cumin
½ teaspoon chilli powder
2 teaspoons chopped rosemary leaves
2 tablespoons olive oil
sea salt and cracked black pepper
white bean hummus* to serve

Preheat the oven to 180°C (355°F). Place the pumpkin, sweet potato and zucchinis in a bowl. Toss the vegetables in the combined paprika, cumin, chilli, rosemary, oil, salt and pepper. Place in a lined baking dish and bake for 40 minutes or until golden. Serve with the hummus and grilled (broiled) flatbread. Serves 4.

asparagus and potatoes with lemon butter

12 baby new potatoes, thickly sliced
24 asparagus spears
1 bunch english spinach, leaves only
lemon butter
90g (3 oz) butter
2 tablespoons lemon juice
2 cloves garlic, sliced

To make the lemon butter, place the butter in a saucepan over low heat. Simmer until golden. Remove from the heat, add the lemon juice and garlic and set aside. Place the potatoes in a steamer over a saucepan of boiling water and cook for 3 minutes. Add the asparagus and steam for a further 2 minutes. Add the spinach and steam for 1 minute, turning once. To serve, place the vegetables on plates and spoon over the lemon butter. Top with a poached egg if desired. Serves 4.

honey roast vegetables on pepper polenta

4 baby fennel, halved
2 carrots, peeled and halved
2 red onions, peeled and halved
1 large orange sweet potato (kumara), peeled and quartered
¼ cup (2 fl oz) honey
1 tablespoon lemon juice
1 tablespoon olive oil
1 cup instant polenta*
4½ cups (2 pints) boiling chicken or vegetable stock
60g (2 oz) butter
sea salt and cracked black pepper
4 thick slices creamy blue cheese

Preheat the oven to 200°C (390°F). Place the fennel, carrots, onions and sweet potato in a baking dish lined with baking paper. Combine the honey, lemon juice and oil and pour over the vegetables. Bake for 40 minutes or until golden. To cook the polenta, have the stock simmering over medium-high heat. Add the polenta in a thin stream and stir for 5 minutes or until it comes away from the sides of the pan. Add the butter, salt and a generous amount of pepper and place on plates. Top with the cheese and vegetables and serve. Serves 4.

root vegetable fritters

½ cup plain (all-purpose) flour
3 eggs, lightly beaten
1 cup grated parsnip
1 cup grated carrot
3½ cups grated sweet potato
½ cup grated parmesan cheese
2 tablespoons chopped flat-leaf parsley
sea salt and cracked black pepper
vegetable oil for cooking
200g (7 oz) soft goat's cheese or fresh ricotta cheese

Place the flour in a bowl. Add the eggs and whisk until smooth. Add the parsnip, carrot, sweet potato, parmesan, parsley, salt and pepper and mix to combine. Heat a large non-stick frying pan over medium heat. Add a little oil and 2 tablespoons of fritter mixture. Flatten the mixture and cook for 2–3 minutes each side or until golden. Repeat with the remaining mixture. Sandwich fritters together with the goat's cheese or ricotta and serve with rocket (arugula). Serves 4.

roast tomato dinner bruschetta

1kg (2 lb) cherry tomatoes, halved
olive oil
salt and pepper
8 slices crusty wood-fired bread
¼ cup basil, roughly torn
½ cup black olives, pitted
8 slices prosciutto*, torn into small pieces
shaved parmesan to serve
¼ cup (2 fl oz) olive oil, extra
2 tablespoons red wine vinegar

Preheat the oven to 180°C (355°F). Place the tomatoes in 2 baking dishes lined with baking paper. Drizzle with oil, salt and pepper and cook for 35 minutes or until the tomatoes are soft and slightly dried. Brush the bread with oil and grill (broil) until golden. To serve, combine the tomatoes with the basil, olives and prosciutto and spoon over the bread. Top with the parmesan. Combine the extra olive oil and vinegar to make a dressing, pour over the bruschetta and serve. Serves 4.

roast tomato dinner bruschetta

puffy cheese and spinach omelette

puffy cheese and spinach omelette

4 eggs, separated
⅓ cup (2½ fl oz) milk
½ cup grated cheddar cheese
sea salt and cracked black pepper
10g (¼ oz) butter
150g (5 oz) baby spinach leaves

Place the egg yolks, milk, cheese, salt and pepper in a bowl and mix to combine. Place the egg whites in a clean bowl and whisk until soft peaks form, then fold through the egg yolk mixture. Heat a 24cm (9½ in) non-stick frying pan over high heat. Add the butter and spinach to the pan and cook for 1 minute or until the spinach is just wilted. Pour over the egg mixture, stir gently to distribute the spinach and cook over low heat for 10 minutes or until the base is golden. Fold the omelette in half onto itself. Serve with hot buttered toast and a simple salad. Serves 2.

VARIATIONS

+ **three cheese** When combining the ingredients for the egg yolk mixture, add 50g (1½ oz) crumbled fetta cheese and 30g (1 oz) crumbled soft blue cheese to the above recipe.

+ **mushroom** Place 20g (½ oz) butter into the frying pan and add 250g (8 oz) sliced medium-sized button mushrooms. When the mushrooms are cooked and golden, remove from the pan, wipe out the pan and continue with the recipe. Add the mushrooms and 1 tablespoon chopped parsley to the omelette just before you fold it over.

+ **bacon** Begin the recipe by frying 4 rashers bacon until crisp. Remove from the pan, wipe out the pan and continue with the recipe. Add the cooked bacon to the omelette just before you fold it over.

pumpkin, onion and blue cheese frittata

148

three baked beans

roast vegetable couscous

pumpkin, onion and blue cheese frittata

1 tablespoon olive oil
2 onions, sliced
750g (1½ lb) pumpkin, peeled and chopped
1 tablespoon thyme leaves
1 tablespoon water
6 eggs, lightly beaten
¾ cup (6 fl oz) milk
150g (5 oz) soft blue cheese, crumbled
cracked black pepper

Heat a 24cm (9½ in) non-stick frying pan over medium heat. Add the oil and onions and cook for 6 minutes or until the onion is soft and dark golden. Add the pumpkin, thyme and water to the pan and cook, covered, for 10 minutes, stirring occasionally, or until the pumpkin is soft. Combine the eggs, milk, blue cheese and pepper and pour over the pumpkin. Cook for 4 minutes or until just set. Place under a preheated hot grill (broiler) and cook until the top is golden. Serve with baby spinach leaves on hot buttered toast. Serves 4.

three baked beans

1 tablespoon oil
2 onions, sliced
4 garlic cloves, sliced
1 tablespoon oregano leaves
sea salt and cracked black pepper
400g (14 oz) can butter beans, drained and rinsed
2 x 400g (14 oz) cans borlotti beans, drained and rinsed
400g (14 oz) can white beans*, drained and rinsed
500ml (16 fl oz) tomato puree
1 cup (8 fl oz) vegetable or beef stock
⅓ cup (2½ fl oz) red wine
1 tablespoon brown sugar

Heat a frying pan over high heat. Add the oil, onions, garlic, oregano, salt and pepper and cook for 5 minutes or until the onions are a light golden colour. Add the butter, borlotti and cannellini beans, tomato puree, stock, wine and sugar and simmer for 10 minutes or until the mixture has thickened. Serve the beans with crisp grilled (broiled) bacon and hot buttered toast. Serves 4.

roast vegetable couscous

2 red capsicums (bell peppers), quartered
4 roma tomatoes, halved
4 field mushrooms
2 tablespoons olive oil
sea salt and cracked black pepper
store-bought tzatziki*
couscous
1½ cups couscous
1½ cups (12 fl oz) hot chicken or vegetable stock
⅓ cup grated parmesan cheese
2 teaspoons finely grated lemon rind
150g (5 oz) baby spinach or rocket (arugula) leaves

Preheat the oven to 200°C (390°F). Place the capsicums, tomatoes and mushrooms in a baking dish lined with baking paper and sprinkle with the olive oil, salt and pepper. Bake for 45 minutes or until the vegetables are tender. To make the couscous, place the couscous into a heatproof bowl and cover with the stock. Cover the bowl with plastic wrap and allow to stand for 5 minutes or until all the liquid has been absorbed. Stir through the parmesan, lemon rind and spinach or rocket. Place the couscous on serving plates. Top with the vegetables and serve with the tzatziki. Serves 4.

spinach pie

2 x 250g (8 oz) packets frozen leaf spinach
1kg (2 lb) fresh ricotta cheese
5 eggs
2 tablespoons chopped dill
sea salt and cracked black pepper
250g (8 oz) cherry tomatoes, halved
150g (5 oz) fetta cheese, roughly crumbled

Preheat the oven to 160°C (320°F). Defrost the spinach in the microwave or in a saucepan over medium heat, then squeeze out all the liquid. Place the spinach in a bowl with the ricotta, eggs, dill, salt and pepper and combine. Spoon the mixture into a 12 cup (4½ pint) capacity ovenproof baking dish. Top with the cherry tomatoes, cut side up, and sprinkle with the fetta. Bake for 1 hour or until the pie is set and slightly golden. Serve warm or cold with a simple salad. Serves 4.

spinach pie

thai red pumpkin curry

1 tablespoon vegetable oil
2 onions, cut into wedges
2 teaspoons grated ginger
1–2 tablespoons thai red curry paste
1 cup (8 fl oz) vegetable stock
400ml (12 fl oz) can coconut milk
1.25kg (2¾ lb) pumpkin, peeled and sliced
4 baby eggplants (aubergines), halved
100g (3½ oz) green beans, trimmed
½ cup basil leaves

Heat a wok or deep frying pan over high heat. Add the oil, onions, ginger and curry paste and cook for 1 minute. Add the stock and coconut milk and bring to a simmer. Add the pumpkin, cover and cook for 5 minutes. Add the eggplants and beans and cook for a further 5 minutes or until the pumpkin is soft. Stir through the basil and serve with steamed rice. Serves 4.

VARIATIONS

+ **squash and asparagus** Add 200g (7 oz) trimmed and halved asparagus and 200g (7 oz) halved yellow squash to the curry instead of the eggplant and beans.

+ **vegetable** Add 300g (10 oz) broccoli florets and 1 thickly sliced red capsicum (bell pepper) to the curry instead of the eggplant and beans.

+ **potato and pea** Replace the pumpkin with 1kg (2 lb) peeled and chopped waxy potatoes and cook for 10 minutes rather than 5. Replace the eggplant with 1 cup frozen peas.

thai red pumpkin curry

eat your greens stir-fry

2 teaspoons sesame oil
2 teaspoons vegetable oil
2 cloves garlic, crushed
2 teaspoons grated ginger
350g (12 oz) broccoli, sliced
150g (5 oz) green or snake beans, trimmed
2 bok choy*, quartered
100g (3½ oz) snow peas (mange tout), trimmed
¼ cup (2 fl oz) hoisin sauce*
¼ cup (2 fl oz) sherry or chinese cooking wine*

Heat a frying pan or wok over high heat. Add the oils, garlic and ginger and cook for 30 seconds. Add the broccoli, beans, bok choy and snow peas and cook for 3 minutes or until the vegetables are just tender. Add the hoisin and sherry or wine and cook for 1 minute. Serve with steamed rice and top with fried tofu if desired. Serves 4.

easy tomato and zucchini lasagne

1kg (2 lb) fresh ricotta cheese
½ cup chopped flat-leaf parsley
½ cup finely grated parmesan cheese
sea salt and cracked black pepper
2 x 400g (14 oz) cans peeled tomatoes, crushed
2 cups (16 fl oz) tomato puree
⅓ cup chopped basil
375g (13 oz) or 8 fresh lasagne sheets
750g (1½ lb) or 5 zucchinis (courgettes), thinly sliced
1¼ cups grated mozzarella cheese

Preheat the oven to 180°C (355°F). Combine the ricotta, parsley, parmesan, salt and pepper to make the ricotta layer. Combine the tomatoes, tomato puree and basil for the tomato layer. To assemble, line the base of a 14 cup (6 pint) capacity ovenproof dish with lasagne sheets. Top with some of the ricotta mixture and zucchini slices, then spoon over some of the tomato mixture to cover. Top with another lasagne sheet. Continue with the layers until all the ingredients are used, finishing with a tomato layer. Top with the mozzarella and bake for 30 minutes or until cooked through and the cheese is golden. Serve with a simple green salad. Serves 4.

eat your greens stir-fry   easy tomato and zucchini lasagne

tomato and eggplant tarts

tomato and eggplant tarts

2 x 85g (2½ oz) frozen shortcrust pastry sheets
¾ cup ricotta cheese
2½ tablespoons chopped basil
⅓ cup grated parmesan cheese
250g (8 oz) cherry tomatoes, halved
3 baby eggplants (aubergines), thinly sliced
olive oil for brushing
sea salt and cracked black pepper

Preheat the oven to 180°C (355°F). Trim the edges of the pastry sheets, then cut each sheet in half. Place the pastry bases on baking trays lined with baking paper. Combine the ricotta, basil and parmesan and spread over the pastry leaving a 1cm (½ in) border. Top the ricotta mixture with the cherry tomatoes, cut side up, and eggplants. Brush with olive oil and sprinkle with salt and pepper. Bake for 20 minutes or until golden. Serve with a simple green salad. Serves 4.

VARIATIONS

+ **tomato and zucchini** Replace the baby eggplants with 2 zucchinis (courgettes) cut into thin slices.

+ **tomato and three cheeses** After spreading the ricotta mixture over the pastry bases, arrange 150g (5 oz) mozzarella slices over the pastry and sprinkle with ⅓ cup extra parmesan cheese before adding the tomatoes. Omit the eggplants.

+ **tomato and asparagus** Replace the sliced eggplants with 10 halved asparagus spears. Top with baby rocket (arugula) leaves and parmesan cheese shavings and serve.

short cuts

peel or no peel?

If you are preparing roast vegetables and are a little short on time, there really is no need to peel them. For pumpkin, potatoes, sweet potatoes and parsnips a quick scrub under the kitchen tap is preparation enough for the pan. If you really don't like the idea of pumpkin skin, it's much easier to cut off after cooking.

switch blades

For time-poor cooks there is no better investment than a quality, sharp vegetable peeler. A good one should glide over the vegetables, ridding them of skins in minutes. Substandard varieties tend to blunt quickly, dragging across the vegetables and making your job much more difficult than it should be.

essential elements

Some of the best standby ingredients you can have in the pantry are cans of vegetables and beans. Keep a stock of white beans and chickpeas (garbanzos), as well as whole peeled tomatoes in your cupboard. Peas, spinach and other frozen vegetables are also great standards to keep on hand.

roast perfection

The secret to great roast vegetables – crunchy on the outside and soft in the middle – is to arrange them properly. Put vegetables that should be really crisp, like potatoes, around the outside edges of the pan and work your way in, with the smaller, quick-cook vegetables, such as pumpkin and onions, in the middle.

sweets

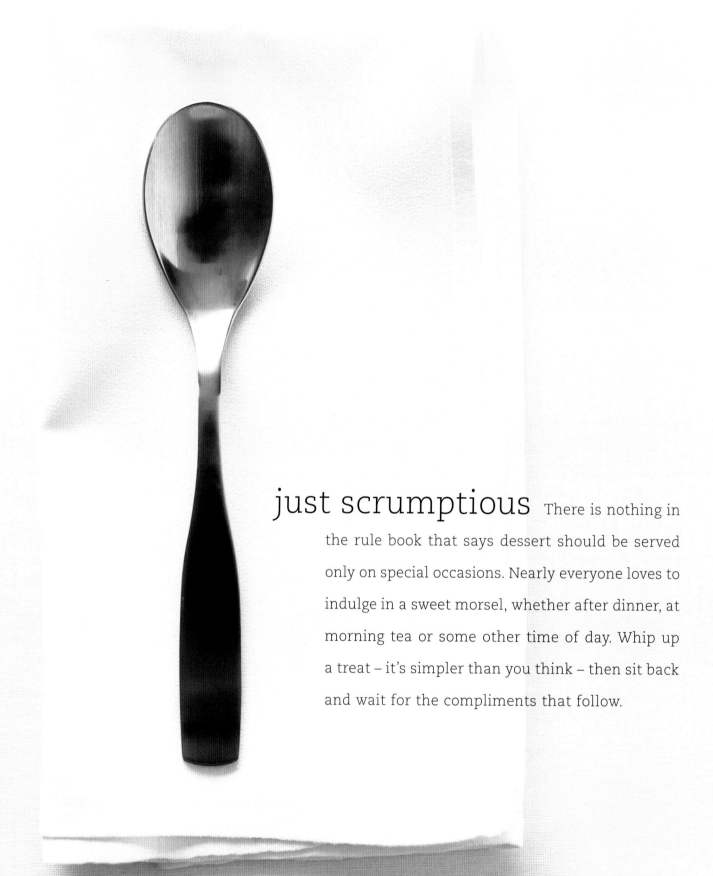

just scrumptious
There is nothing in the rule book that says dessert should be served only on special occasions. Nearly everyone loves to indulge in a sweet morsel, whether after dinner, at morning tea or some other time of day. Whip up a treat – it's simpler than you think – then sit back and wait for the compliments that follow.

blueberry and white chocolate mousse

mango with lime and vanilla syrup   raspberry bread and butter puddings

melon and sorbet with mint sugar

blueberry and white chocolate mousse

3 tablespoons water
2 teaspoons gelatine powder
150g (5 oz) white chocolate, chopped
2 cups (16 fl oz) (single or pouring) cream
1 cup blueberries

Place the water in a bowl and sprinkle the gelatine over it.
Stand until the gelatine absorbs the water. Place the chocolate
and cream in a saucepan over medium-low heat. Stir until
smooth. Add the gelatine mixture and stir for 1 minute to
dissolve. Remove from the heat and place the mixture in
a bowl. Whisk for 3 minutes or until cooled. Stir through the
blueberries and pour into 6 x 1 cup (8 fl oz) capacity greased
serving glasses. Refrigerate for 45–60 minutes to set. Serve
with extra blueberries if desired. Serves 6.

mango with lime and vanilla syrup

1 cup (8 fl oz) water
⅔ cup sugar
2 tablespoons lime juice
1 vanilla bean*, split
4 mangoes, cheeks removed and peeled

Place the water, sugar, lime juice and vanilla bean in a small
saucepan over low heat. Stir until the sugar is dissolved.
Increase the heat and boil for 7 minutes or until slightly
thickened. Set aside to cool. Spoon over the mango cheeks
to serve. Serves 4.

raspberry bread and butter puddings

soft butter for spreading
12 slices bread, crusts removed
200g (7 oz) frozen raspberries
custard
2 eggs, lightly beaten
1 cup (8 fl oz) milk
1 cup (8 fl oz) (single or pouring) cream
⅔ cup icing (confectioner's) sugar
1 teaspoon vanilla extract

Preheat the oven to 160°C (320°F). Butter half the bread and
sandwich together with the remaining slices. Cut the sandwiches
in half. Divide the sandwiches between 4 x 1 cup (8 fl oz)
capacity greased ramekins, placing the raspberries between
the layers of sandwiches. To make the custard, combine the
eggs, milk, cream, sugar and vanilla and whisk to combine.
Pour over the bread and allow to stand for 5 minutes. Place
the ramekins in a baking dish and fill with enough hot water
to come halfway up the sides of the ramekins. Bake for
35 minutes or until just set. Makes 4.

melon and sorbet with mint sugar

½ cup sugar
¼ cup finely chopped mint leaves
4 slices rockmelon (cantaloupe)
store-bought sorbet of your choice
4 slices honeydew melon

Place the sugar and mint in a food processor and process until
well combined. To serve, place the rockmelon slices on serving
plates and top with scoops of sorbet and a slice of honeydew
melon. Sprinkle with the mint sugar and serve. Serves 4.

simple rhubarb tart

8 thin or 4 halved thick stalks rhubarb
2 tablespoons caster (superfine) sugar
1 sheet ready-prepared puff pastry*
1 cup ricotta cheese
2 tablespoons icing (confectioner's) sugar
1 teaspoon vanilla extract

Preheat the oven to 200°C (390°F). Place the rhubarb on
a baking tray lined with baking paper. Sprinkle with the sugar.
Bake for 20 minutes or until soft, then allow to cool. Trim the
edges of the pastry and place on a baking tray lined with
baking paper. Place the ricotta, icing sugar and vanilla in a
bowl and mix to combine. Spread the mixture over the pastry,
leaving a 1cm (½ in) border. Top with the cooked rhubarb
and fold over the border edges to form a crust. Place in the
oven and bake for 12–15 minutes or until the filling is set
and the pastry is golden. Serve warm or cold. Serves 4.

simple rhubarb tart

apricot upside-down syrup cakes

apricot upside-down syrup cakes

90g (3 oz) butter
1¼ cups brown sugar
3 tablespoons water
12 apricots, halved and stoned
cake
75g (2½ oz) butter
½ cup caster (superfine) sugar
2 eggs
1 cup hazelnut meal*
1 cup plain (all-purpose) flour
1 teaspoon baking powder
⅓ cup (2½ fl oz) milk

Preheat the oven to 160°C (320°F). Place the butter, sugar and water in a saucepan over medium heat and stir until the butter is dissolved to make a caramel syrup. Add the apricots and cook for 2 minutes. Spoon the apricots and some of the syrup into the base of 6 x 1 cup (8 fl oz) capacity greased non-stick muffin tins. Reserve the remaining syrup for serving. To make the cake, place the butter, sugar, eggs, hazelnut meal, flour, baking powder and milk in a bowl and mix until combined. Spoon the cake mixture over the apricots. Bake for 25 minutes or until cooked when tested with a skewer. Cool in the tins for 5 minutes and then invert onto serving plates. Serve with the extra caramel syrup and thick (double) cream. Makes 6.

VARIATIONS

+ **mango** Replace the apricots with 2 peeled and thickly sliced mangoes. Replace the hazelnut meal with 1 cup desiccated coconut.

+ **blackberry and almond** Replace the apricots with 300g (10 oz) defrosted frozen blackberries. Replace the hazelnut meal with 1 cup almond meal.

+ **apple** Replace the apricots with 2 sliced green apples. Replace the hazelnut meal with 1 cup almond meal.

chocolate french toast

toasted sponge cake with pears

macaroon ice-cream sandwiches

chocolate french toast

16 slices soft baguette
100g (3½ oz) dark chocolate, melted
2 eggs, lightly beaten
⅓ cup (2½ fl oz) milk
2 tablespoons icing (confectioner's) sugar, sifted
butter for frying
icing (confectioner's) sugar, extra, for dusting

Spread half the baguette slices with the melted chocolate and
sandwich together with the remaining slices. Combine the
eggs, milk and icing sugar, then dip the sandwiches into the
mixture. Cook in a large buttered frying pan over medium heat
for 2 minutes each side or until golden. Serve warm and
dusted with icing sugar. Serves 4.

toasted sponge cake with pears

8 thick slices sponge cake
50g (1½ oz) melted butter
1 tablespoon white sugar
2 pears, sliced
sugar, extra
⅓ cup (2½ fl oz) dessert wine
thick (double) cream to serve

Brush both sides of the cake slices with a little melted butter
and sprinkle with the sugar. Heat a non-stick frying pan over
high heat. Add the cake slices a few at a time and cook for
30 seconds each side or until golden. Place on serving plates.
Press both sides of the pear slices into the extra sugar and
cook for 1–2 minutes each side or until golden. Set aside.
Add the dessert wine to the pan and cook for 30 seconds.
To serve, drizzle the cake slices with a little dessert wine
and top four of the slices with the cream and pears and the
remaining four slices of cake. Serves 4.

macaroon ice-cream sandwiches

3 cups desiccated coconut
3 egg whites
¾ cup caster (superfine) sugar
good-quality vanilla ice-cream
good-quality chocolate ice-cream

Place the coconut, egg whites and sugar in a bowl and mix
until combined. Place 2 tablespoon quantities of mixture well
spaced on baking trays lined with baking paper. Press each
with the back of a spoon to flatten. Bake at 180°C (355°F)
for 7 minutes or until light golden. Cool on the trays. To serve,
place a macaroon on each serving plate and top with a couple
of scoops of vanilla or chocolate ice-cream and another
macaroon. Makes 10.

caramel banana tarte tatin

80g (2½ oz) butter
⅓ cup brown sugar
1 tablespoon (single or pouring) cream
3 bananas, sliced lengthwise
1 sheet ready-prepared puff pastry*

Preheat the oven to 200°C (390°F). Place the butter, sugar
and cream in a 22cm (9 in) ovenproof frying pan. Stir the
mixture over medium heat until the sugar has melted and the
caramel is simmering. Remove from the heat and add the
bananas, cut side down, to fit over the base of the pan. Cut
out a rough circle of pastry to fit on top of the bananas, place
over and bake for 20 minutes or until the pastry is puffed and
golden. Stand for 5 minutes before inverting onto a serving
plate. Serve with thick (double) cream or ice-cream. Serves 4.

caramel banana tarte tatin

tiramisu

1¾ cups (14 fl oz) (single or pouring) cream
500g (1 lb) mascarpone*
1 cup (8 fl oz) coffee liqueur
2 cups (16 fl oz) espresso coffee
26 store-bought sponge finger biscuits*
cocoa powder for dusting

Place the cream in a bowl and whisk until soft peaks form. Fold through the mascarpone and set aside. Combine the liqueur and coffee. Quickly dip both sides of half the biscuits in the coffee mixture and use them to layer the base of a 10 cup (4 pint) capacity serving dish. Spoon half the cream mixture over the layer of biscuits. Dip the remaining biscuits, place on the cream layer and spoon over the remaining cream mixture. Dust the top with cocoa and refrigerate for at least 1 hour before serving. Serves 8–10. This is also great made the day before serving.

VARIATIONS

+ **raspberry and dessert wine** Replace the coffee liqueur and espresso with 1 cup (8 fl oz) dessert wine. Layer 600g (20 oz) defrosted frozen raspberries with the biscuits and cream mixture.

+ **rum and raisin** Place 2 cups raisins and ⅓ cup (2½ fl oz) rum in a small saucepan over low heat. Cook for 2 minutes or until the liquid is absorbed. Set aside to cool. Replace the coffee liqueur with an extra ⅓ cup (2½ fl oz) rum and layer the raisins with the biscuits and cream mixture.

+ **chocolate** Melt 330g (11 oz) dark chocolate with 1 cup (8 fl oz) (single or pouring) cream over low heat, stirring until smooth. Set aside to cool to room temperature. Spoon the chocolate mixture over the biscuits before topping with the cream mixture.

tiramisu

chocolate dessert cakes

simple choc hazelnut layer cake

lemon puddings

chocolate dessert cakes

185g (6 oz) butter, melted
1 cup caster (superfine) sugar
⅓ cup brown sugar
3 eggs
1¼ cups plain (all-purpose) flour
1 teaspoon baking powder
1 cup cocoa
vanilla bean ice-cream or thick (double) cream to serve

Preheat the oven to 160°C (320°F). Place the butter, sugars and eggs in a bowl and mix until combined. Sift over the flour, baking powder and cocoa and mix until combined. Place in 4 x 1 cup (8 fl oz) capacity ovenproof tea or coffee cups and bake for 20 minutes or until fudgy. Serve warm or cold in the cups topped with some ice-cream or cream. Serves 4.

simple choc hazelnut layer cake

2 x 20cm (8 in) quality store-bought sponge cakes
1 cup chocolate hazelnut spread
topping
1¼ cups (10 fl oz) thick (double) cream
¼ cup icing (confectioner's) sugar
1 cup chocolate hazelnut spread

Cut each sponge cake into 3 layers. Spread each layer thinly with the chocolate hazelnut spread and sandwich together. To make the topping, place the cream, icing sugar and chocolate hazelnut spread in a bowl. Fold gently to combine and spread over the top and sides of the cake. Serves 8–10.

lemon puddings

90g (3 oz) soft butter
1½ cups caster (superfine) sugar
1½ cups (12 fl oz) milk
3 eggs
½ cup (4 fl oz) lemon juice
½ cup plain (all-purpose) flour
1 teaspoon baking powder

Preheat the oven to 180°C (355°F). Place the butter, sugar, milk, eggs, lemon juice, flour and baking powder in a food processor and process until smooth. Pour the mixture into 6 x 1 cup (8 fl oz) capacity greased ramekins or ovenproof teacups and bake for 20–25 minutes or until golden. Serve warm with vanilla ice-cream. Serves 6.

cheat's apple tarts

1½ sheets ready-prepared puff pastry*
60g (2 oz) butter, melted
1 tablespoon sugar
3 apples, cored and thinly sliced
½ teaspoon cinnamon
2 tablespoons brown sugar
1 tablespoon lemon juice

Preheat the oven to 180°C (355°F). Brush the pastry sheets with the butter and cut into six pieces. Press into 6 x 1 cup (8 fl oz) capacity greased muffin tins, discarding the excess pastry. Sprinkle with the sugar. Combine the apples, cinnamon, brown sugar and lemon juice and divide between the pastry cases. Bake for 20 minutes or until the apples are soft and the pastry is golden and crisp. Serve warm with cream or vanilla ice-cream. Serves 6.

cheat's apple tarts

short cuts

the crème de la cream

Thick or double cream tastes delicious served with all sorts of sweets and desserts. It also has the edge over whipped cream when it comes to presentation, as it holds its peaks much better. Whipped cream tends to lose the air you've churned into it and becomes a little watery unless used straightaway.

berry delicious

Keep an assortment of frozen berries on hand. When you're making cakes or muffins there isn't even a need to defrost them – in fact, your baked goods will turn out better if you leave the berries frozen. They're also handy to add to a bowl of yoghurt or a smoothie, as they only take about 5 minutes to thaw.

let them eat cake

If there isn't enough time to bake a cake from scratch, you can still give one the personal touch. Buy plain cakes, such as sponges or chocolate cakes, from the local patisserie or supermarket and then finish them at home. All you need do is ice them or sandwich them together with cream and jam.

making a crust

You'll be prepared for unplanned desserts if you keep sheets or blocks of ready-prepared puff and shortcrust pastry in the freezer. Pies and tarts can be made in double-quick time when all you have to do for the shell is roll out the pastry. The topping can be as simple as spoonfuls of jam or thinly sliced fruit.

glossary

arborio rice
Has a short, plump-looking grain with surface starch which, when cooked to al dente in risotto, creates a cream with the stock. Substitute with carnaroli rice.

balsamic vinegar
This Italian vinegar, although tart like other varieties, has a less astringent taste and more of a rich, red wine flavour. Like some wines, the older a balsamic vinegar is, the better it tastes.

basmati rice
A long-grained white rice that is aromatic and firm in texture.

blanching
A cooking method that heightens the flavour and colour of certain foods and makes them more tender. It involves plunging food, such as vegetables, into boiling unsalted water for a few seconds or minutes, then removing and refreshing under cold water.

blood orange
Variety of orange with sweet flesh that ranges from bright red to ruby red.

bocconcini
Fresh Italian mozzarella balls, usually made from cows' milk. Sold in a whey liquid at supermarkets and delicatessens.

bok choy
A mildly flavoured green vegetable, also known as chinese chard or chinese white cabbage. Baby bok choy can be cooked whole after washing. If using the larger type, separate the leaves and trim the white stalks. Limit the cooking time so that it stays green and slightly crisp.

capers
The small, deep green flower buds of the caper bush. Available packed either in brine or salt. Use salt-packed capers when possible, as the texture is firmer and the flavour superior. Rinse thoroughly before use.

chinese cooking wine
Sold in Asian food stores – often labelled 'shao hsing' – this blend of glutinous rice, millet, a special yeast and the spring waters of Shao Hsing in northern China is similar to dry sherry.

chinese five-spice powder
This combination of cinnamon, anise pepper, star anise, clove and fennel is excellent with chicken, meats and seafood. It is sold in Asian food stores and most supermarkets.

chorizo
Firm, spicy, coarse-textured Spanish pork sausage seasoned with garlic and paprika. Available from delicatessens and some butchers.

couscous
The name given to both the national dish of Algeria, Tunisia and Morocco and the tiny grains of flour-coated semolina that are used to make it. Available from supermarkets.

cream
Pouring cream (also called single or medium cream) is referred to in this book as 'cream'. It has a butterfat content of 20–30 per cent. Thick or double cream, which is thick enough to be spoonable, has a butterfat content of 45–55 per cent.

fish sauce
An amber-coloured liquid drained from salted, fermented fish and used in Thai dishes. Available from supermarkets and Asian food stores, where it is often labelled 'nam pla'.

haloumi
Firm white Middle Eastern cheese made from sheeps' milk. It has a stringy texture and is usually sold in brine. Available from delicatessens and some supermarkets.

hazelnut meal
Available at many supermarkets. Make your own by processing whole skinned hazelnuts to a fine meal in a food processor or blender (130g/4 oz whole hazelnuts will give 1 cup hazelnut meal). To remove the skins from whole hazelnuts, wrap in a tea towel and rub vigorously.

hoisin sauce
A thick, sweet Chinese sauce made from fermented soybeans, sugar, salt and red rice. Used as a dipping sauce or marinade and as the sauce with Peking duck. Available from Asian food stores and most supermarkets.

kaffir lime leaves
Fragrant leaves used crushed or shredded in Thai-style dishes. Available fresh or dried in packets from Asian food stores and some greengrocers.

laksa paste
Purchase good quality laksa paste from Asian food stores or make your own.

6 large red chillies, seeded and chopped
2 teaspoons shrimp paste*
⅓ cup dried shrimp
2 onions, chopped
1 tablespoon grated ginger
2 stalks lemongrass, chopped
1 teaspoon ground turmeric
1 tablespoon ground cumin

Place all the ingredients in a blender or food processor and blend until smooth. Refrigerate for up to 2 weeks. Makes ½ cup.

lemongrass
Aromatic grass that is popular in Thai cooking as it gives a spicy, lemony flavour. Sold fresh in Asian food stores.

mascarpone
A fresh Italian triple-cream curd-style cheese. It has a similar consistency to thick (double) cream and is often used in the same way. Available from specialty food stores and many delicatessens and supermarkets.

miso paste
A Japanese paste made of fermented soybeans and rice. It comes in a variety of strengths distinguished by the colour: generally, the darker the colour, the stronger the miso. Available from Asian food stores and many supermarkets.

mizuna
A green Japanese vegetable related to cabbages and turnips. The long leaves, used mainly in salad mixes, have a distinct mustard-like taste.

noodles

egg noodles
Made from wheat flour and eggs, these yellow-coloured noodles are available fresh or dried in a variety of thicknesses. They are commonly used in stir-fries and soups.

fresh rice noodles
Available in a variety of thicknesses, including thin, thick and rolled, from Asian food stores and some supermarkets. Only use fresh noodles that are a few days old at most. Soak in boiling water for 1 minute, then drain.

hokkien noodles
Round yellow noodles made of wheat and available from the refrigerator section of most supermarkets and Asian food stores. To use, place the noodles in a bowl, cover with boiling water and soak for 1–2 minutes. Stir the noodles once to separate, then drain.

rice vermicelli noodles
Fine, ready-cooked, dry noodles. Soak them in boiling water for a short time, drain, then combine with other ingredients.

nori
Dried seaweed pressed into square sheets and used in Japanese-style dishes. Available from Asian food stores.

oyster sauce
A Chinese sauce made from oysters, soy sauce, salt and spices. Available from Asian food stores and supermarkets.

polenta
Used extensively in northern Italy, this corn meal is cooked in simmering water until it has a porridge-like consistency. In this form it is enriched with butter or cheese and served with meat dishes. Otherwise it is left to cool, cut into squares and either grilled, fried or baked. Available from delicatessens and most supermarkets.

prosciutto
Italian ham that has been salted and air-dried for up to 2 years. The paper-thin slices are eaten raw or used to flavour cooked dishes. Also known as parma ham. Substitute with thinly sliced smoked bacon.

puff pastry
Because it is so time-consuming to make, many cooks choose to use ready-prepared puff pastry. It can be ordered in advance from patisseries in blocks or bought from the supermarket in both block and sheet forms. If buying sheets of puff pastry you may need to layer several to get the desired thickness.

pumpkin
Many varieties are available, but I prefer to use these for my recipes.

butternut pumpkin
Cylindrical pumpkin with smooth, light yellow skin and sweet, dry orange flesh. Use for baking, stuffing or mashing.

jap pumpkin
Has a green-and-white striped skin and moist, soft, bright-orange flesh with a sweetness that intensifies with cooking.

ramekins
Small overproof dishes usually made from porcelain and used to cook dishes such as soufflé and crème brûlée that are served individually.

red curry paste
Buy good-quality pastes in jars from Asian food stores or the supermarket, or make your own.

3 small red chillies
3 cloves garlic, peeled
1 stalk lemongrass, chopped
4 green onions (scallions), chopped
1 teaspoon shrimp paste*
2 teaspoons brown sugar
3 kaffir lime leaves*, sliced
1 teaspoon finely grated lemon rind
1 teaspoon grated ginger
½ teaspoon tamarind concentrate
2–3 tablespoons peanut oil
Place all the ingredients except the oil in the bowl of a small food processor or spice grinder. With the motor running, slowly add the oil and process until you have a smooth paste. Refrigerate in an airtight container for up to 2 weeks. Makes ½ cup.

rice flour
A fine flour made from ground white rice. Used as a thickening agent, in baking and to coat foods when cooking Asian dishes.

salted capers
See capers.

scoring
A method of preparation that involves running the point of a sharp knife over the surface of meat or seafood in a cross-hatch formation so that it cuts about halfway through. Commonly used when preparing squid hoods for frying.

shrimp paste
Also known as blachan, this strong-smelling paste is made from salted and fermented dried shrimps pounded with salt. Used in South-East Asian dishes, it should always be fried before use. Keep well sealed in the fridge. Available from Asian food stores.

sponge finger biscuits
Sweet, light, finger-shaped Italian biscuits, also known as savoiardi. Great for desserts such as tiramisu because they absorb other flavours and soften well while still maintaining their shape. Available from delicatessens and most supermarkets.

star anise
Strong aniseed-flavoured seed cluster shaped like an eight-point star obtained from a tree in the magnolia family. Used in Asian cooking, either whole or ground as a spice. Available from Asian food stores and some supermarkets.

stock
Flavoured, strained liquid obtained by simmering meat and bones with vegetables and herbs.

beef stock
1.5kg (3 lb) beef bones, cut into pieces
2 onions, quartered
2 carrots, quartered
2 stalks celery, cut into large pieces
assorted fresh herbs
2 bay leaves
10 peppercorns
4 litres (8 pints) water
Cook the bones in a 220ºC (425ºF) oven for 30 minutes. Add the onions and carrots and cook for 20 minutes. Transfer bones, onions and carrots to a stockpot or large saucepan. Add the remaining ingredients. Bring to the boil and simmer for 4–5 hours, skimming regularly. Strain the stock and use, or refrigerate for up to 3 days or freeze for up to 3 months. Makes 2.5–3 litres (5–6 pints).

chicken stock
1.5kg (3 lb) chicken bones, cut into pieces
2 onions, quartered
2 carrots, quartered
2 stalks celery, cut into large pieces
assorted fresh herbs
2 bay leaves
10 peppercorns
4 litres (8 pints) water
Place all the ingredients in a stockpot or large saucepan. Simmer for 3–4 hours, skimming regularly. Strain and use, or refrigerate for up to 3 days or freeze for up to 3 months. Makes 2.5–3 litres (5–6 pints).

vegetable stock
4 litres (8 pints) water
1 parsnip
2 onions, quartered
1 clove garlic, peeled
2 carrots, quartered
300g (10 oz) cabbage, roughly chopped
3 stalks celery, cut into large pieces
small bunch fresh mixed herbs
2 bay leaves
1 tablespoon peppercorns

Place all the ingredients in a stockpot or large saucepan and simmer for 2 hours, skimming regularly. Strain and use, or refrigerate for up to 4 days or freeze for up to 8 months. Makes 2.5–3 litres (5–6 pints).

tahini
A thick, smooth, oily paste made from toasted and ground sesame seeds. Available in jars from health food stores and most supermarkets.

tzatziki
Refreshing Greek dip made from yoghurt, chopped cucumber and garlic. The Turkish version is called cacik.

vanilla bean
The pod of an orchid vine native to Central America. It is added, either whole or split, to hot milk or cream to allow the flavour to infuse. Available from specialty food stores, supermarkets and delicatessens.

wasabi paste
A pungent traditional Japanese condiment made from horseradish. Available from Asian food stores.

white beans
These small, kidney-shaped beans are also often called cannellini beans. Available from delicatessens and supermarkets either in a dried form, which needs to be soaked overnight before using, or canned.

white bean hummus
2 x 440g (14½ oz) cans white beans, rinsed and drained
2 tablespoons lemon juice
1 tablespoon tahini*
sea salt
Place the ingredients in a food processor and process until smooth.

conversion chart

1 teaspoon = 5ml
1 Australian tablespoon = 20ml
  (4 teaspoons)
1 UK tablespoon = 15ml
  (3 teaspoons/½ fl oz)
1 cup = 250ml (8 fl oz)

liquid conversions

metric	imperial	US cups
30ml	1 fl oz	⅛ cup
60ml	2 fl oz	¼ cup
80ml	2¾ fl oz	⅓ cup
125ml	4 fl oz	½ cup
185ml	6 fl oz	¾ cup
250ml	8 fl oz	1 cup
375ml	12 fl oz	1½ cups
500ml	16 fl oz	2 cups
600ml	20 fl oz	2½ cups
750ml	24 fl oz	3 cups
1 litre	32 fl oz	4 cups

cup measures

1 cup almond meal	110g	3½ oz
1 cup breadcrumbs, fresh	50g	2 oz
1 cup sugar, brown	200g	6½ oz
1 cup sugar, white	225g	7 oz
1 cup caster (superfine) sugar	225g	7 oz
1 cup icing (confectioner's) sugar	125g	4 oz
1 cup flour, plain (all-purpose)	125g	4 oz
1 cup rice flour	100g	3½ oz
1 cup rice, cooked	165g	5½ oz
1 cup arborio rice, uncooked	220g	7 oz
1 cup basmati rice, uncooked	220g	7 oz
1 cup couscous, uncooked	180g	6 oz
1 cup lentils, red, uncooked	200g	6½ oz
1 cup polenta, fine, uncooked	180g	6 oz
1 cup basil leaves	45g	1½ oz
1 cup coriander (cilantro) leaves	40g	1¼ oz
1 cup mint leaves	35g	1¼ oz
1 cup flat-leaf parsley leaves	40g	1¼ oz
1 cup cashews, whole	150g	5 oz
1 cup cooked chicken, shredded	150g	5 oz
1 cup olives	175g	6 oz
1 cup parmesan cheese, finely grated	100g	3½ oz
1 cup green peas, frozen	170g	5½ oz

index

donna hay is an Australian-based food stylist, author and magazine editor and one of the best-known names in cookbook and magazine publishing in the world. Her previous seven books have sold more than two million copies internationally and are renowned for their fresh style, easy-to-follow recipes and inspirational photography. These best-selling, award-winning titles – *modern classics book 1* and *book 2*, *off the shelf* and *marie claire cooking* (*The New Cook*), *dining* (*Entertaining*), *food fast* (*New Food Fast*) and *flavour* (*Flavors*) – together with *donna hay magazine*, have revolutionised the way we think about, prepare and enjoy food.